TRIAL *of*
FAITH

TRIAL *of* FAITH

Why a lawyer abandoned
his **MORMON** faith,
argued against it,
and RETURNED TO DEFEND IT

DUSTY SMITH
KIMIKO CHRISTENSEN HAMMARI

CFI
An imprint of Cedar Fort, Inc.
Springville, Utah

This is not an official publication of The Church of Jesus Christ of Latter-day Saints. The opinions and views expressed herein belong solely to the author and do not necessarily represent the opinions or views of Cedar Fort, Inc. Permission for the use of sources, graphics, and photos is also solely the responsibility of the author.

ISBN 13: 978-1-4621-2262-2

Published by CFI, an imprint of Cedar Fort, Inc.
2373 W. 700 S., Springville, UT 84663
Distributed by Cedar Fort, Inc., www.cedarfort.com

LIBRARY OF CONGRESS CATALOGING-IN-PUBLICATION DATA

Names: Smith, Dusty, 1960- author. | Hammari, Kimiko Christensen, author.
Title: Trial of faith : why a lawyer abandoned his Mormon faith, argued
   against it, and returned to defend it / Dusty Smith and Kimiko Christensen
   Hammari.
Description: Springville, Utah : CFI, An imprint of Cedar Fort, Inc., [2018]
   | Includes bibliographical references.
Identifiers: LCCN 2018027176 (print) | LCCN 2018031515 (ebook) | ISBN
   9781462129409 (epub, pdf, mobi) | ISBN 9781462122622 (perfect bound : alk.
   paper)
Subjects: LCSH: Smith, Dusty, 1960- | Ex-church members--Church of Jesus
   Christ of Latter-day Saints--Biography. | Mormon converts--Biography. |
   Lawyers--Biography. | LCGFT: Autobiographies.
Classification: LCC BX8695.S475 (ebook) | LCC BX8695.S475 A3 2018 (print) |
   DDC 289.3092 [B] --dc23
LC record available at https://lccn.loc.gov/2018027176

Cover design by Wes Wheeler
Cover photo © 2018 Scott Jarvie
Cover design © 2018 Cedar Fort, Inc.
Edited by Deborah Spencer and Melissa Caldwell
Typeset by Kaitlin Barwick

Printed in the United States of America

10 9 8 7 6 5 4 3 2 1

Printed on acid-free paper

I would like to dedicate this work to my mom, who believed in me; my dad, who inspired me; my children, Joshua, Brittany, and Matt, for filling my heart with love; and my wife, Susan, who saved my life, changed my existence, and melted my heart.

I also dedicate this work to all who search, struggle, and doubt. May you keep your eyes focused on Heavenly Father.

Contents

Preface

I can't remember a time when I didn't believe in God or love Him. When I joined The Church of Jesus Christ of Latter-day Saints in 1983 at the age of twenty-three, I was ecstatic to have found the truth. I served a mission and then got married and started a family, but too many unanswered questions led to the loss of my testimony. I became anti-Mormon in every way imaginable and used my skills as an attorney to prove to people that the Church was wrong.

After twenty-six years of rabid hatred toward the Church, my heart softened, and I was baptized into The Church of Jesus Christ of Latter-day Saints for the second time. The same God whom I loved as a child, and whom I never stopped believing in, showed me miracle after miracle and brought me home.

This book is about my journey of finding the truth, losing my testimony, fighting against the truth, and then returning to the church that I had hated for so long. It's about God's love for His children and His knowledge about the most intimate details of our lives.

In October 2017, *LDS Living Magazine* wrote an article about my story. Since then, I have been interviewed by several other media outlets and have spoken at dozens of firesides across the United States. To date, my story has reached about one million people, and I hope it continues to spread—not because I want fame or glory, but because I love the Lord and love sharing my testimony. I want others to know Him the way I do. I want people to know that God loves them and has a plan for them, that we have a living prophet today who guides us. I now know with all my heart that the Church is true, and I want others to know the same.

Since my story went viral on the internet, I have received more than a thousand emails and Facebook messages from people who have been touched by my story. Many of those people have asked to hear more about my story, and others have asked me how to handle certain doubts. That is why I have written this book—to share my story in hopes that it will lead others to Christ. This book is divided into two parts. Part one discusses my conversion, my falling away and becoming anti-Mormon a few years later, and my reconversion. In part two, I cover some of the common gospel questions people have asked me about why we need a prophet, how to overcome doubts, and how they can see miracles like I have.

As you read this book, you may have questions about my first wife and my children. However, I have chosen not to discuss them in detail. This book is about my story and my journey, and I have purposely omitted facts about my family out of respect for their privacy. I hope you will offer them the same respect by focusing on my conversion and God's love for His children, rather than on any unanswered questions you may have about my family.

Most of all, I hope this book will spark in you a desire to be closer to Heavenly Father and Jesus Christ. If you consider yourself a strong, active member of the Church, I hope you will continue on that path. If you have doubts, I hope this book will inspire you to pray and receive the answers you're seeking. If you have no testimony at all or even have angry feelings toward the Church, I hope you will find peace.

I know that God lives, that His Son, Jesus Christ, died for us, and that Joseph Smith was a true prophet who restored the true Church of Jesus Christ. May you find that same knowledge and feel the overwhelming love our Heavenly Father has for you. He has blessed me more than I could have ever imagined, and I know He is ready to bless you too.

Foreword

By Mike Robertson

March 16, 2015, started out just like every other day. After getting out of bed, saying my prayers, and then reading my scriptures, I opened my laptop and began working. My phone buzzed, and I answered with a cheery "hello." The voice on the other end of the line didn't respond but simply started to bear the most incredible testimony that I have ever heard. Not because it was somehow different, but because of who was bearing it. My heart swelled. I could feel in an unmistakable way the truthfulness of what was being said. The Spirit was so strong that my whole body was enveloped with an indescribable love. I began to sob like a baby, and tears streamed down my cheeks. It was a day I will never forget.

Who could have ever imagined that this day would come at our first meeting? I had first encountered the voice on the other end of the line sixteen years earlier in a computer chat room called "What Do Mormons Really Believe?" He came to the room with the screen name Atticus taken from the book *To Kill a Mockingbird* from the attorney character, Atticus Finch, and he was there to tell us what we "really" believed. I'm sure, in his own way, he actually believed everything that he was saying, even though most of it was untrue. You could really feel the bitterness, hate, and betrayal coming from his words. But there was also something different. Even in the hate, there was a sense of love for the Lord. Clearly the light of Christ had not left his heart. I used to picture Atticus as Saul in the New Testament. A person who really thought he was doing what God wanted, but at the same time doing all the wrong things. Maybe that was how I could withstand the onslaught of accusations and false doctrines thrown out as questions or statements of belief. Many of these I had also never heard before, even though I had grown up in Utah and been a member of the Church my whole life. When this happened, I would spend hours and even days researching records and trying to find truth. I always came up with a totally different answer than Atticus and would politely answer the question or relay the real truths on each and every subject that he brought up. Over time, we began to develop a close friendship, and I began to tell him that one day he would be back. His answer was always the same, and sometimes he used words I cannot repeat, but I would smile and let him know I had put his name on the temple prayer roll that week. While I knew that one day he would be back, I wondered if it would be on this or the other side of the veil.

That is one reason Dusty's story is so compelling. It is a story of hope. A story of love and compassion and finally coming to the truth. It is a story not only of love for the Lord, but of the love the Savior has for each of us no matter what state we find ourselves in. It is a story of never giving up. Our Father in Heaven never gives up on us, and He is always there, with open arms outstretched to receive us. And it is a story of Father sending angels from both sides of the veil to help us in our times of need. There are miracles in everyone's lives all the time if we just look for them. Whether you have lost your testimony of the gospel of Christ or you are struggling with points of doctrine or policies of the Church, or if you have loved ones who have, this book is for you.

PART I

My Story

Introduction

The Lord's hand is guiding you. By "divine design," He is in the small details of your life as well as the major milestones.[1]

—Ronald A. Rasband

At the beginning of 2015, I was a successful attorney in Dallas, Texas, a devout Catholic, and a former Latter-day Saint who was once a vocal anti-Mormon. Six months later, I was an unemployed Latter-day Saint living in an apartment in Salt Lake City. I'd sold my house and left my job with no other motive than God had told me to do it. A year later, President Dieter F. Uchtdorf told my story in general conference and ordained me a high priest.

This timeline seems insane, and I still marvel at that whirlwind year. But looking back, I know it wasn't a whirlwind. My life changed quickly in the months before my baptism, but I know God had been preparing me for twenty-six years—actually my entire life—for that moment.

When God wants something, He makes it happen. I've learned not to question Him. He knows what's best for us and is acutely aware of the intricate details of our lives. He doesn't control us the way a puppeteer manipulates a marionette, but He does put us in the right place at the right time so we can find the greatest happiness.

It's not a coincidence that I grew up with a mother and grandparents who loved God and taught me how to serve Him. It's not a coincidence that I went to a Lutheran school as a boy and became a Bible scholar. Nor is it a coincidence that my mother received a copy of the Book of Mormon during a business trip and that the same book fell off the bookshelf when I was looking for something to read.

I don't believe in coincidences. Elder Neal L. Maxwell said, "*Coincidence* is not an appropriate word to describe the workings of an omniscient God. He does not do things by 'coincidence' but . . . by 'divine design.'"[2] I believe in divine design and miracles—the times God intervenes to help us—but I don't believe in coincidences.

My journey back to the The Church of Jesus Christ of Latter-day Saints was certainly a miracle. In fact, it consisted of many miracles that God wove into a beautiful tapestry with His divine design. Without Him I would be nothing, for He has been guiding me my entire life. Even when I turned my back on Him, He never turned His back on me. Even when I persecuted the Church and fought to destroy it, God poured out His love on me and fought to bring me back.

On April 23, 2015, I joined The Church of Jesus Christ of Latter-day Saints for the second time. As I entered the waters of baptism, I knew this time would be different. It had to be. I walked toward my friend Steve Marsh, who was instrumental in helping me get to that point, and let go of years of anger and bitterness. Where so much anger and hatred once lived in my heart, I now felt peace and love. I'd spent decades fighting against the Church, but none of that mattered anymore. I'd found my way home. I may have lost my battle to prove the Church wrong, but I'd won in every other way.

I looked up at Steve, who would perform this sacred ordinance, and saw my life flash before me. In just a few moments my old life would be over. I would start over as the person I once was decades before, only this time I'd fight harder to defend the Church and help bring others unto Christ.

NOTES

1. Ronald A. Rasband, "By Divine Design," *Ensign*, Nov. 2017.
2. As quoted in ibid., italics in original.

Chapter 1

Humble Beginnings

Your present circumstances don't determine where you can go; they merely determine where you start.[1]

—Nido Qubein

When I was five years old, I learned about broken families, broken hearts, and broken promises. That was the year my dad left. I wish I knew more about him, yet I remember enough. My memories of him have molded me into the man I am today. I've learned that some promises get broken, but I can make my own promises and choose to keep them. And we all have a Father in Heaven who will never let us down.

My biological father wasn't a very nice person when he drank. And he liked to drink. I still remember how mean and scary he became when he drank too much. After he would finish with his drunken outbursts, my mother would hold me and say, "It's not you. It's the alcohol. He loves you. It's the alcohol." But actions often speak louder than words, and as a little boy I could not understand my father's intentions. I knew I never wanted to be an alcoholic like him. At only five years old, I knew it could ruin my life. I promised my mother I would never touch alcohol, and I never have.

*Even at the age of five, I had a great respect for the
military and wanted to wear the uniform.*

It hasn't always been easy. Whether it was my friends in high
school, classmates in college, or my family members at reunions,
everyone seemed to be drinking. Everyone except me. At times, I
felt a little left out, but for the most part, people respected my decision. I was still adamant about not becoming like my dad when he
drank. And when I got older and learned that alcoholism can be
hereditary, I was too scared that if I took the first drink, I wouldn't
be able to stop.

Little did I know at the time how much this promise was preparing me to make even greater promises later in life. I didn't even
realize until years later that other people choose not to drink and
that sobriety is one of God's commandments. It wasn't a coincidence that I made a pledge to my mother at such a young age. The
Lord was preparing me to receive the gospel. In fact, I don't believe
there was ever a time that He wasn't preparing me for something.
There were times when I wasn't listening—and definitely times

when I turned my back on the truth—but God never stopped loving me and preparing me to get back on the right path.

Although I didn't have The Church of Jesus Christ of Latter-day Saints when I was a boy, I knew God and was surrounded by people who loved Him. My mother was Lutheran, my grandmother was Baptist, and my grandfather was Catholic. None of them ever missed church, and I dutifully attended with each of them. Because my mother was Lutheran, I considered myself Lutheran as well, but I frequently went to Baptist services with my grandmother or to Mass with my grandfather.

I had a good understanding of all three churches, but I didn't understand why my family all went to different churches. Nor did

My Lutheran confirmation when I was eleven years old.

I understand why all the churches used the Bible but interpreted it differently. I didn't know which church was right or what I needed to do—should I kneel, stand, sprinkle, dunk?

No one was able to answer my questions. At times I would ask my mom or grandparents why we all went to different churches.

"We just like to do things a little differently," they'd tell me. "But in the end we're all worshiping the same God."

Their answers never satisfied me, but I loved God and wanted to serve Him. I continued going to church and reading the Bible and praying with my mom each morning. I attended Lutheran elementary school and wanted to be a minister when I grew up. When I was only six years old, I sang a solo, "What Child Is This?", at our church's Christmas Eve service. I was always participating at church and served as a youth counselor at a church camp when I was a teen. In junior high, I even won first and second place in state Bible knowledge contests sponsored by the Lutheran schools.

If knowing God makes a person rich, then my family was rich. But by the world's standards, we were poor. I grew up in a trailer park in Austin, Texas, and when I was nine, we moved the trailer to some land out in the country near Austin. My mom worked all day and well into the night to provide for the family. My grandparents took care of us when my mom was at work, and I think of them more as second parents than grandparents. I never called them Grandpa and Grandma. To me they have always been Daddy Roy and Momma Lu.

My mom would drop us off at my grandparents' house early in the morning and pick us up at ten that night. I know her absence was out of love and devotion, and I'll always remember the first Christmas without my dad. Even though I was only five, I could sense that times were tough. I believed in Santa Claus, but for some reason I only asked for a sheriff's badge. Santa Claus came through in a big way that year. Not only did I receive the sheriff's badge, but I also got a gun holster and a race car track. I got so much more than I had asked for. Years later I learned that my mom had worked three jobs because she knew Christmas would be hard without my dad, and she wanted to make it special.

My mom taught me by example about working hard and being my best self. She never pushed me to be a certain way, but she also encouraged me to follow my dreams. She loved and accepted me for who I was and wanted others to do the same. When I was in elementary school, the teachers discovered I was left-handed and tried to make me right-handed. My mother marched down to the school and told them they would not try to change me.

Being a single mother in the 1960s wasn't easy, but she always made sure we had what we needed. In 1968, my mother remarried. Robert Sanderfer was a good man, but he and I were never close.

My mother always worked a full-time job, but she always made sure I got to football practice, drama practice, and all my other activities. We never had much money, but she made sure I never felt deprived.

When I was in high school, I wanted to go to the prom but didn't have enough money to take my date to a nice restaurant before the dance. My mom went to McDonald's and set a table with linen, fine china, and crystal. She took on the role of a waitress and served my date and me hamburgers. It was one of the finest meals I've ever eaten.

My mom loves our country as much as she loves God and our family. Both her father and brother served in the military, and she flew the US flag every day at our home. She taught me the Pledge of Allegiance, the American's Creed, and "The Star-Spangled Banner." She taught me the Bill of Rights and told me to fight for them and stand up for them. She made me believe it was our duty to serve in the military, and I eventually became a Lieutenant Colonel in the Army.

My mom may be serious when it comes to God and country, but she has an amazing sense of humor and can be mischievous. Once, after I broke my foot and was on crutches, I went with her and her friend to the mall. She and her friend let me get about a hundred feet ahead of them even though I was on crutches. Then my mom fell against her friend and yelled, "Young man! Bring back my crutches!"

There is no finer woman than my mother. She is my hero and friend. She has held me when I've cried, encouraged me when I've been down, and pushed me when I've needed pushing. I have been told I am a success. If that is true, it is because of her. If it is not, it is because of me.

It's no surprise that my mother is such an incredible woman. She came from incredible parents. Daddy Roy and Momma Lu are some of the finest people to have ever walked the earth.

The first words that come to mind about my grandma are "fire and brimstone." She was a feisty, no-nonsense woman with a sharp, sharp tongue. People tell me I get my quick wit from her. She loved God and the commandments and never missed a day of church until the end of her life. She and Daddy Roy both lived into their nineties and were married more than sixty years. Despite her feistiness, she was also one of the most loving people I have ever met, and my successes can also be attributed to her.

Daddy Roy was my hero. He was a man among men. He never said much; he didn't have to. But when he talked, everyone listened. When he walked into a room, you knew he was there. He just had a presence about him.

I loved spending time with him. I remember sitting on his lap and falling asleep while watching *Gunsmoke*. He would let me tag along with him when he was a ham radio operator, and I would sit and listen to him talk to people all over the world. When I had my first loose tooth, he got some thread and yanked it out. However,

This is my favorite picture of my maternal grandparents.

he pulled the wrong tooth, and I ended up with two teeth for the tooth fairy.

He enlisted in the Army when he was young and later became an officer. He joined the Air Force when it was formed and retired as a Major.

I spent my life trying to make him proud of me. When I joined the Army, I showed up at his house in Austin wearing my uniform. When he walked into the room, I stood at attention for him.

He said only three words: "Shine your shoes." Then he walked away.

"What about my belt buckle?" I hollered after him.

Momma Lu said, "If your buckle needed shining, he would have told you."

Years later, Momma Lu told me that one of his proudest moments was when I became the first in my family to graduate from college. He was even prouder when I graduated from law school. He never told me. He never said much, but I knew how much he loved me.

As I stated earlier, I was never close to my first stepdad, Bob Sanderfer. We watched football and worked together building on to the trailer to make it a house, but we didn't play catch or do the typical things that fathers and sons do. I never heard from my biological father, and his absence sparked a fire in me to be the best at everything. I wanted to make him regret leaving me.

I was naturally smart, athletic, and talented in singing and acting. I loved performing and was involved in several plays. I was also good at sports and played football until I injured my back in high school and couldn't play anymore. My natural talents combined with my competitive drive helped me excel in almost everything I tried.

No one in my family had gone to college, but I always knew I'd go. It just seemed to be part of who I was. It didn't matter that no one else had gone or that we didn't have the money to go. I knew it would be mostly up to me to get there, and I was okay with that. I knew I would find a way.

I raised dogs and sold them to earn money. That was about all I could do as a boy out in the country since I couldn't mow neighbors' lawns. My mom supported me in this endeavor and helped me put money into a savings account for college.

The day I turned sixteen, I started working in gravel pits to earn money for college. Sometimes it was hard when my friends were off playing football and enjoying being kids, but I had a goal and would do anything to achieve it.

I received college scholarships for the Lutheran ministry and for acting, but I turned them down. By then I wasn't sure if the Lutheran church was the right church, and I didn't want to commit to a life as a minister. Although I still loved performing, I turned down the acting scholarship because going to law school and becoming a lawyer was my new dream.

In high school, I read *To Kill a Mockingbird* and decided I wanted to be Atticus Finch when I grew up. Not only did I love his demeanor in the courtroom, but I admired his character in general. He was such a stand-up guy who loved his family and community and would do anything to help them. To him it didn't matter that he would most likely lose his case with Tom Robinson, the black man he was defending. He knew representing him was the right thing to do and that he'd be a hypocrite to his children if he didn't give all he had to proving Tom Robinson was innocent. He explained this to his daughter, Scout, and then added, "Simply because we were licked a hundred years before we started is no reason for us to try not to win."[2]

Atticus knew he was going to lose, yet he tried anyway. He gave his heart and soul to the case and showed that a decent human being looks beyond race and social status and looks out for the welfare of others.

In some ways I, too, was licked a hundred years before I started. I grew up in a trailer without my father. No one in my family had ever gone to college, and no one in my family could afford to help me pay for it. But I knew that wasn't a reason not to try. I knew that I could be like Atticus and rise above the opposition.

My outcome was very different from Atticus's. I won my "case." I went to college and, against all odds, graduated in four years with a degree in public relations. Atticus may have lost his case, but in my eyes he still won. He showed his community what it means to have integrity, to fight for the right with the ferocity of a dragon, even when no one believes in you. Atticus may be a fictional character, but he became one of my heroes. I knew I wanted to spend my life emulating him and defending people's honor.

My college experience was not like my peers'. Because I turned down the scholarships, I had to work full time to pay my own way and didn't have time for parties or extracurricular activities. I enrolled in ROTC because I always knew I'd serve my country someday, but I was appalled by the hazing taking place. It was crude and immature, and I didn't want any part of it. Leaving

ROTC meant giving up another scholarship, but my morals and reputation were more important to me than money.

Working my way through college was definitely difficult, but I wasn't afraid of hard work. If my mom could work three jobs while raising a family without a husband, then I could work while going to school. I worked at least forty hours a week, sometimes as many as fifty or sixty. To save money on rent, I lived in a dorm room on the fourth floor with no elevator or air conditioning. I went to class from eight until noon and then worked until nine or ten at night. I had several different jobs that I did on different days of the week. If I wasn't singing in a night club, then I was waiting tables or delivering food or telegrams. I usually had Friday nights off, but then I'd have to get up early on Saturday to work again.

I no longer went to church on Sundays. During my sophomore year, my relationship with God changed. A thirteen-year-old girl, who was a family friend, was killed unexpectedly. She was running home from school and thought the glass door was open, but it was actually shut. She ran through the door, the door shattered, and a

One of my many jobs in college was singing in a night club.

piece of glass pierced her neck. She died instantly. I was angry at God. How could He let someone like that die? She was such a good kid with her whole life in front of her, and now she was dead. Why didn't He protect her?

I decided that if that was how God treated people who loved Him, then I was done with Him. I never stopped believing in Him, but I was angry and bitter and wanted nothing to do with Him. I kept my distance from Him by not reading the scriptures and not attending church. But, as I would see over and over again throughout my life, God never kept His distance from me.

NOTES

1. https://www.brainyquote.com/quotes/nido_qubein_178331
2. Harper Lee, *To Kill a Mockingbird* (New York: Popular Library, 1962), 101.

Chapter 2

Finding the Truth

*I may not have ended up where I intended to go, but
I think I have ended up where I needed to be.[1]*

—*Douglas Adams*

After graduating from the University of Texas at Austin, I couldn't find work in my field right away, so I accepted a job as an assistant manager at Wendy's. Working in the fast food industry definitely wasn't my dream, but I was grateful for a job and for the opportunity to work in management. Later I found a job doing PR for an ice cream company. When I felt like it was time to move on from that job, I went to the Texas Employment Commission to look at job openings in the Austin area. They ended up hiring me to help others find jobs. Though I still had a dream of becoming a lawyer, I wasn't sure when or if that would happen. Law school was so expensive, and I didn't have the money to go. I felt I had no choice but to work and make money and hope that somehow I could someday achieve my dream of becoming an attorney.

One day around that time, I went home to my parents' house to do laundry. It seemed like an ordinary day with ordinary tasks before me. Little did I know that my entire life was about to change.

Graduating from the University of Texas at Austin.

I decided to find something to read while I washed my clothes and went into my old bedroom to find a book. My mom had rearranged some things when I left for college, so not all of the books in my old bedroom were mine. When I pulled a book off of the shelf, a Book of Mormon was stuck to it and literally fell off the shelf. My mom had been to Salt Lake City on business, and someone had given her a Book of Mormon.

Curious, I opened it to Third Nephi and read about Jesus Christ visiting the American continent. *This is pretty cool*, I thought to myself. I was surprised that Jesus had visited this land, but it all made sense. I immediately felt a pull to learn more.

I went to the phone book and looked up The Church of Jesus Christ of Latter-day Saints. For a boy who was raised Catholic and Lutheran, the listings for "wards" and "stakes" meant nothing to me. I didn't know which number to call, but because it was lunch-time and I was hungry, I decided to call a stake.

A man who I later learned was the stake president answered the phone. After we exchanged hellos, he said, "I'm never here at lunchtime, but I forgot something and I came to pick it up. What can I help you with?"

"I'd like to learn more about your church," I told him.

"Is this a joke?" he asked.

"No," I replied. "I'm serious."

"I'll tell you what," he said. "Give me your address, and I'll send the missionaries to you."

"No," I said. "Tell me where to meet them and I'll go meet them."

"Now I know this is a joke," he said.

I explained to him that I lived out in the country and it would be easier for me to meet the missionaries in the city. When he was finally convinced that this wasn't a joke, he set up an appointment for me with the missionaries.

I met with the missionaries that afternoon at the university ward in Austin. I was their golden contact, and from the beginning, everything they taught me made sense. They used the Bible quite a bit, so I didn't feel like they were trying to take away from what I already knew about God and Jesus Christ. They were simply adding to what I had learned as a boy. And the Book of Mormon seemed to only add to what the Bible taught. I read it as often as I could and took it to work to read during my lunch hour. Not once did I find that it contradicted the Bible or introduced completely new teachings. As its subtitle states, it is truly "another testament of Jesus Christ." It didn't take long for the Holy Ghost to bear witness to me that not only was this the church for me, but it was also the true church of Jesus Christ.

I loved learning about the Word of Wisdom. Finally I knew there were people like me who didn't drink, and I could be myself around the members of the Church and not feel ridiculed. I also liked that they didn't smoke or drink coffee because I didn't like those things either. Before meeting with the missionaries, I had never thought coffee was bad; I just didn't care for it.

Most important, I finally got the answer to my question of why there were so many churches and why they all taught different things. I learned that there had been an apostasy after Jesus died and that for almost two thousand years the true church was not on the earth. In the 1800s, Joseph Smith was called as a prophet to restore the Lord's true church. Until then, none of the churches on the earth had the proper authority to perform ordinances such as baptism. Those churches may have taught about Jesus and had good intentions, but they lacked priesthood authority. The missionaries pointed out the scripture in Ephesians that says there is "one Lord, one faith, one baptism" (4:5). It made complete sense. There is only one God, so wouldn't there be only one church and one set of teachings?

I was excited to learn that God continued to call prophets after Joseph Smith and that there was a living prophet on the earth. It only made sense since the Old Testament prophet Amos had taught, "Surely the Lord God will do nothing, but he revealeth his secret unto his servants the prophets" (3:7). Why would God speak to the people of one dispensation but not another?

My testimony was further strengthened when the missionaries taught me about the restoration of the Melchizedek Priesthood. Hearing about Peter, James, and John giving Joseph Smith the Melchizedek Priesthood triggered memories of a reoccurring dream I had in elementary school. In that dream I could see the heavens open and the clouds part. Three men, who I somehow knew were Peter, James, and John, were dressed in robes and carrying walking sticks. They seemed to be listening to someone who was giving them instructions. When they were finished, they climbed down a ladder through a hole in the clouds and came to earth.

I had that dream almost every night when I was a boy. It took about fifteen years to finally make sense. After talking to the missionaries, I knew for a surety that Peter, James, and John had given Joseph Smith the Melchizedek Priesthood. I realized God had been speaking to me since I was a child and preparing me to accept the truth. And now He was speaking to me again and telling me that The Church of Jesus Christ of Latter-day Saints had the complete truth.

I was baptized after only a few weeks on April 30, 1983. My mother didn't attend because she was in the hospital recovering from foot surgery. My stepdad came, although probably against his will, and told me that no one in the family would ever accept me being a Latter-day Saint. Later he told me that no one in the family would ever accept me being a missionary either. I don't remember my mom ever saying anything negative, but I felt she wasn't pleased with my decision to be baptized. My relationship with my family became strained. We didn't lose complete contact, but we spoke less often, and our conversations felt forced.

I also lost my girlfriend, who was Baptist and couldn't accept my new religion. And yet, I didn't feel completely alone. I had new friends in the Church, and of course I had God. Most important, I met Dean Hall.

Dean had recently returned from his mission, and when we met, I felt like I had known him forever. We bonded like family. We were inseparable. Soon, I was going home with Dean for Sunday dinner. His parents, Lewis and Karen Hall, accepted me as their own. Being with the family gave me a crash course on what it was like to be a member of the Church. I had brothers and sisters. I received monthly father's counsels and father's blessings. Eventually I moved in with the Halls. They accepted me as part of their family, and to me Lewis and Karen were Father and Mother. My mom and I were still "us," but the Lord knew what I needed in my life at that time.

*With the Hall family boys. This family "adopted" me
after I was baptized and took me in as their own.*

Two months after getting baptized, I was asked to speak in stake conference. I agreed to do it, not understanding the magnitude of that responsibility. I had been attending the university ward, which didn't have a typical meetinghouse. We met in a big room on the college campus and sat on folding chairs. During the week, the room was used to host ward parties and other events. The first time I went to a typical LDS meetinghouse was when I spoke in stake conference. The chapel and overflow section were packed, but I wasn't nervous. I'd given enough speeches and performed enough growing up that the crowd didn't faze me.

I had just been given the Aaronic Priesthood and opened my talk with a joke, playing on the word *Aaronic.* "I was just given the priesthood, which is pretty ironic because I was going to be a minister when I was a Lutheran." The congregation laughed, and I continued with my conversion story, bearing witness of the great love that God has for each of us.

After I was baptized, people started bugging me.

"You need to go on a mission," they'd say.

"I'm not going on a mission," I'd adamantly declare. I wasn't nineteen. I was twenty-three and a college graduate. I had a full-time job and a fiancée. It was time for me to be an adult and start the rest of my life.

People continued to hound me, and I continued to tell them I would never go.

And then, one day in February 1984, I was sitting in sacrament meeting at the university ward, and I got an undeniable impression that I needed to serve a mission. It was so powerful that I walked out of the meeting and went straight to the bishop's office. I called Father (Lewis Hall).

"Are you sitting down?" I asked him. He said no, and I told him he should probably sit down.

"Will you buy my car?" I said.

"Buy your car? Why?" he asked.

"Because I need to sell it before I go on my mission."

"You're going on a mission?" was all he managed to say. He was shocked, but I was too. I'd only made this decision a couple minutes earlier, and a couple minutes before that I was sure I'd never serve a mission. It's amazing how quickly your life changes when you follow the Spirit.

I put my paperwork in right away, and my call arrived on April 19, 1984. Mother brought me the letter at work, and I met her in the parking lot. Understanding that I wanted to open my mission call in private, she smiled, wished me luck, and drove away. I opened my call alone in the parking lot. I knew I would go wherever the Lord called me, but I had prayed to go foreign and to speak Spanish. I didn't know Spanish at the time, but I was exposed to it frequently living in Texas and wanted to learn the language and teach the Hispanic people. I was ecstatic when I read the words,

"You have been assigned to labor in the Honduras Tegucigalpa Mission." We don't always get what we pray for, and other times the Lord gives us exactly what we ask for. I was grateful that He had heard my prayers and had fulfilled both of my requests.

At the time of my call, I was working as an assistant manager in the men's department at Montgomery Ward. I had come across the job opening when I was working at the Texas Employment Commission, and I had decided to apply for it. I was able to use my employee discount at Montgomery Ward to buy my suits and the other clothes I would need for my mission.

This is one of the many examples of how God put me in the right place at the right time. If I hadn't been working at the Texas Employment Commission, I may not have seen the job opening at Montgomery Ward and wouldn't have gotten my mission clothes at such a good price. Some people may argue that it was just clothes and God doesn't care about trivial matters. But I know He does. He cares about everything we do because He loves us.

God showed me another miracle when my doctor forgave a large debt. I had had eye surgery the year before and still owed the doctor several hundred dollars for what my insurance didn't cover. I told the doctor I was going on a mission and asked him if we could postpone the payments until I returned.

"You're going on a mission?" he said.

"Yes," I said.

I didn't mention the name of the church, and he didn't ask. He simply said, "If you're going to be a missionary, then I'm going to waive the bill."

It was apparent that God wanted me to go on a mission and was opening the way for me. When He wants you to be someplace, He makes sure you get there. But that doesn't mean it wasn't hard and I didn't doubt my call at times.

The MTC was a strange experience for me. I wasn't like the other missionaries there. I hadn't been a member of the Church all my life. I didn't have parents who supported and encouraged my decision. And I wasn't nineteen.

I was twenty-four by then, and much of the time I felt like I was light years ahead of the other missionaries in age and life experiences. Many of them had never lived away from home, and at night they'd roughhouse in the hallways and run around. That wasn't my thing, and sometimes I felt like I was babysitting.

My family didn't want me to be there. My fiancée also wasn't excited I was there, even though she was also a member of the Church. I decided that if no one wanted me to serve a mission, then I had no reason being there.

One day, I finally had enough. But I needed to tell someone I was done. Not knowing whom else to tell, I decided to go straight to the top. I went to a pay phone and dialed Church headquarters.

A lady answered the phone and I told her, "Nobody cares that I'm a missionary. I may as well go back home. Nobody wants me to be here."

"Could you hold, please?" she asked.

A few minutes later a man came on the phone. "Elder," he said, "my name is L. Tom Perry. If nobody else cares, I do."

We then chatted for several minutes. He inquired about my background, my family, my age, my status. He was surprised I was twenty-four. He was further surprised that I was the only member of the Church in my family. He listened intently and kept asking questions. I started to believe he actually *did* care! At the end of the conversation, he asked me to be his pen pal. Elder Perry wrote to me my entire mission and even asked to meet me in his office when I returned home. He understood my situation and knew that missionary service would be a struggle at my age. His letters were full of encouragement, and I treasure the words that helped me face my challenges.

When I left the MTC and arrived in Honduras, I was shocked at the living conditions there. It was my first time being in a

*With my companion and another set of
missionaries in my first area, Progreso.*

third-world country. I thought my family was poor, but these
people were truly poor. Of course there were rich people with nice
houses, but the majority of the people I worked with lived in shacks
made of scraps of wood and metal. They had dirt floors, and the
people would sweep them every morning to remove the loose dirt
so that only the smooth hard-packed dirt remained.

The climate was hot and humid, and I never felt clean. We were
blessed to have running water, but it was dirty. My companion and
I would put a sock over the showerhead to filter out some of the
dirt, but it didn't filter everything. We drank this water too, and I
always seemed to be getting sick. Once I had kidney stones, and it
seemed like I always had diarrhea or migraines. I lost about thirty
pounds over the course of my mission and looked like I had a ter-
minal disease when I returned home.

The physical conditions were difficult, but the loneliness I felt
was even greater. Not only was I dealing with the age gap between

my companions and me, but I was far from home with limited communication with my family. In the 1980s, we didn't have the internet, so we had to rely on the postal service, which was completely unreliable and unpredictable in Honduras. Sometimes I went weeks or months without receiving a letter. My mom sent me cookies for my birthday in July, and I didn't receive them until December. Of course, they weren't edible by then. Other times, I received mail with great anticipation, only to learn that my parents were getting divorced or that my fiancée was breaking up with me.

My life seemed to be falling apart. I was losing everything. I sacrificed eighteen months of my life, which felt like a much greater sacrifice at my age because I also gave up a budding career. I had little support from my family, although I was grateful to still be in contact with them, and now I had lost both my stepdad and the woman I loved.

Serving as a district leader in Talanga, Honduras.

Despite these losses, I knew I was doing the Lord's work and that nothing else mattered. In Matthew 16:25, the Savior promises, "Whosoever will save his life shall lose it: and whosoever will lose his life for my sake shall find it." If I hadn't gone on my mission, I may have been able to save parts of my life. I wouldn't have had to sacrifice my career and probably would've married my fiancée. I could have surrounded myself with colleagues I considered my equals, rather than mission companions who sometimes felt like kids. But that doesn't mean that life would've been easy or perfect. I'm sure I would have faced other trials. And I would've lost all of the blessings that came from my missionary service.

Instead, I chose to lose myself in the service of my Heavenly Father and Jesus Christ. I lost important relationships and opportunities because of it. But as promised in the book of Matthew, I found my life. I found my purpose, I found joy, and I found Christ. Nothing can compare to the experiences I had on my mission and the love I felt from my Heavenly Father. Nothing. I will always look back on my mission as containing some of the greatest days of my life.

While my personal life was falling part, my spiritual life improved by leaps and bounds. I focused on the people I taught and on learning more about the word of God. I diligently studied the scriptures, and my testimony grew. I read books such as *Jesus the Christ* and *The Articles of Faith* several times. One day, my mission president gathered us at the stake center and told us to find a comfortable spot. He said we were going to spend the day reading the Book of Mormon from cover to cover. I don't know how many other missionaries completed this challenge, but I was excited about it and lost myself with Nephi in the wilderness and with Mormon in his solitude after all of his people were killed in the war. I read the Book of Mormon in one sitting and gained a deeper understanding and testimony of it.

God blessed me immensely while I was on my mission. If success is measured by the number of baptisms, then I had a lot of success. And if the definition of a miracle is seeing the hand of God in your life, then I saw miracles every day.

Before my mission, I had a dream that I would baptize someone in a river. I told my mission president about it, but he told me that wasn't going to happen. He explained that every area I'd be in would have a baptismal font. But in my second area, this dream was fulfilled. The water went out right before a baptism, and we couldn't fill the font. There was a river behind the church, and we had the baptism in the river, just like in my dream.

I also remember my first December in Honduras. It was so interesting to experience Christmas in a different culture. We scheduled seven baptisms on Christmas Day. We all met at the little chapel and performed the baptisms. As we stood there, all

Before my mission, I had a dream that I was baptizing someone in a river. In my second area, that prophecy came true.

dressed in white, my companion said, "We have just had a white Christmas."

It seemed as if we saw miracle after miracle. One day while my companion and I were out walking, a man came out of his house and stopped us. Although not a member of the Church, he recognized us as missionaries and asked us to bless his children, who had malaria. I admit I didn't want to. What if the blessing didn't heal these children? Would the parents blame the Church? I reluctantly agreed but prayed fervently in my heart that God would pull through and heal these children.

My companion and I followed the man into the house and found the children in an untidy bed. The children were lethargic and were sweating profusely from their fevers. Their heads were so hot that we almost burned our hands when we gave them the blessing.

A couple days later, my companion and I were walking by their house, and I wanted to check on the children. Still filled with fear that they hadn't been healed, I didn't want to knock on the door. Instead we peeked through the window and saw an empty bed. Grief consumed me, and my heart sank. I was absolutely devastated. Why hadn't God healed these precious children? Why did they have to die?

And then we heard some voices coming from behind the house. We went to check them out and saw the children we had blessed. They were playing soccer! Just two days before, they had been on their deathbeds, and now they were playing soccer. Despite my doubts, despite my fears, God healed them. I received a very powerful reminder that day that God hears and answers prayers.

My mission was full of experiences like this, and I have cherished them all my life. Even when I left the Church and had such hostile feelings against it, I still loved my mission.

I never wanted to work in the mission office or be a zone leader and spend much of my time traveling. I wanted to tract, to teach, to spend my days testifying. My mission president was wonderful and was understanding of my desires. We talked about how I was older than the other elders and could use my skills in management to be a leader. But I didn't want that. I served as a district leader a couple of times, but I didn't want a calling beyond that. I wanted to be in the field, among the people. Teaching them brought me the greatest joy.

NOTE

1. Douglas Adams, *The Long Dark Tea-Time of the Soul*, as quoted in "A Quote from *The Long Dark Tea-Time of the Soul*," *Goodreads*, accessed May 19, 2018, https://www.goodreads.com/quotes/3278-i-may-not-have-gone-where-i-intended-to-go.

Chapter 3

Life after My Mission

Life begins at the end of your comfort zone.[1]

—*Neale Donald Walsch*

Like all faithful missionaries, I went home a different man. Although my body was thin and frail from all of the sickness I had endured, my mind and spirit had never been stronger. My testimony was rock solid, and I left my mission determined to move forward in the gospel and live a life worthy of entering the celestial kingdom someday.

I flew home to Idaho Falls, where the Halls were living. There I would be released from my mission. But first, I was fortunate enough to see my mom, who flew from Austin, Texas, and met me for lunch in New Orleans, Louisiana, the first stop of my flight from Honduras. Afterward we flew to Dallas together before parting ways. She flew back to Austin, and I flew to Salt Lake City, Utah, and then to Idaho Falls, Idaho.

My plane landed in Idaho at two in the morning. I was exhausted upon returning to the Halls' house but refused to go to bed until I could be officially released from my mission the next morning. It just seemed wrong for me to sleep in the United States when I was not released from my calling. I spent some time chatting with the family and then forced myself to stay awake just a few more hours. When morning came, I went across the street to the bishop's house and was released from my mission.

After spending a couple weeks with the Halls, I flew back to Texas. While on my mission, I had discovered that the LSAT (law school admission test), which was only given a few times a year, would be conducted right after my mission. I considered waiting until the next test a few months away. That would give me some time to study and prepare for the LSAT. But if I waited, I would not have my scores back in time to enter law school that September. So, two weeks after my mission, I took the test without any preparation. Then I returned to Honduras to court the woman who would become my first wife. She was a member of the Church and lived in one of the areas where I had served. We were only friends when I was on my mission, but my mission president knew her and had given us permission to write during my mission.

We were soon married and planned to move back to the United States. However, we had to wait several months for her visa to be approved. While we waited, I taught fourth grade. I actually skipped fourth grade when I was in elementary school, so I finally went to fourth grade at the age of twenty-six. I loved teaching and loved the students. Though more than thirty years have passed, I'm still in touch with a few of them.

While in Honduras, I also applied to law schools in the United States. My mom called me one day and said I had been accepted to Thomas M. Cooley Law School in Michigan. Cooley had gotten my information from my LSAT scores. I hadn't heard of the school, but my mom said she had done some research and had learned that it was the only law school that allowed students to work while going to school. No other law school does that, especially not for first-year students. I would have to work if I planned on going to law school, so I knew that I would attend law school in Michigan if I decided to go.

*After my mission, I returned to Honduras and taught
fourth grade. I love being an attorney, but the most
satisfying job I have ever had was being a teacher. These
kids were the best and will be "my kids" forever.*

But I still wasn't sure what to do. I had several options. The principal at the elementary school in Honduras wanted me to continue teaching the following year. Or I could go to Ricks College (now BYU–Idaho) or Brigham Young University in Provo, Utah. My mission president had helped arrange scholarships for me at both schools, and I entertained the idea of getting a second bachelor's degree. Or I could go to law school.

In my heart I knew I wanted to chase my dream of becoming a lawyer, but I was scared. I had never failed at anything in my life, and in my situation, flunking out of law school seemed like a real possibility. I knew I would do fine if I were single and just had to worry about myself, but I had a family to support. I had a wife and now a baby on the way, and on top of that, my wife couldn't drive or speak English. I knew that if I went to law school, not only would I have to work full time, but I would also have to do all the grocery shopping, go to all the doctor's visits, and do all of the other tasks that required a car or communicating with someone. Everything would be left up to me. I started to doubt that I could do it all.

My wife finally got her visa, and we moved to Idaho Falls to be near the Halls. I got a job and spent some time weighing my options.

It's funny. I didn't get my answer about law school from a burning in my bosom or another revelation from the Spirit. I got it while watching a chick flick called *Ice Castles*, a movie about a competitive figure skater named Lexie. Lexie's career is taking off, but then she has an accident and goes blind. Her father doesn't want to her to skate anymore, but her friend tries to convince him that it's right for her.

"It's pointless and cruel," her father says.

"Don't give me that," her friend says. "Not trying is pointless and cruel. Not trying is wondering your whole life if you gave up too soon."[2]

That statement shook my soul to the core. I knew had to try. I didn't want to forgo law school and wonder my whole life if I had given up too soon. I knew what I had to do. I would face my fears and rise to the challenge. If I failed, at least I could say I had tried.

My wife and I packed up everything we owned and drove to Michigan, where we had no family, no friends, no job, and even no home. All I had was a strong conviction that I was supposed to go to a law school that I couldn't afford, and I was terrified.

One morning, after a long drive halfway across the country, we pulled into Lansing, Michigan, and headed straight to the law school. I found a newspaper stand in the foyer of the building and then went back to the car and immediately started looking for an apartment. We found a place we liked, and I soon found a job in telephone sales. I hated it, but it paid the bills, and I had a wife and a child on the way to support.

One day when I was in class, I read in the law school newspaper that tuition would be increasing the next semester. I was furious. I was already having a hard enough time making ends meet, and now they wanted to raise tuition.

I marched over to the administration building and asked to speak to the president of the law school, Thomas Brennan, a former chief justice of the Michigan Supreme Court. His door happened to be open, and I heard him ask the secretary if that was a student asking to see him. She said yes, and he told her to send me in.

"Have a seat," he told me. "What's on your mind?"

"I'm angry at you," I told him plainly.

"Okay," he said. "Why?"

"Because I'm poor. It's hard enough for me to make ends meet, and now you're raising tuition."

He leaned back in his chair and put his fingertips together, the same way a bishop sometimes does when he's interviewing some-one. He smiled at me and said, "Well, I can't lower the tuition, but there's one thing I can do."

"What's that?"

"Come work for me." Apparently he was impressed with my attitude.

I worked for him for a year doing odd jobs. If he needed a special project done for the law school, I would do it. Sometimes I helped him recruit students. Whatever he needed, I did it.

After a year, he told me, "I can't do anything for you anymore. Your job isn't helping you, but I know a judge that I went to law school with. He's a judge in Jackson, Michigan, and he needs a clerk. I put in a good word for you. Go interview with him."

I worked with Judge Britten for the next three years until I finished law school and joined the Army. I was his bailiff and law clerk. Each morning I drove an hour to Jackson and worked from eight to five. Then I rushed back to Lansing for classes. I attended law school classes from six until ten and then studied from ten until two. I slept for three hours, woke up at five, studied, and then drove the hour back to Jackson to work. Somehow I also had to find time to go grocery shopping, take my wife to the doctor, and attend to anything else she couldn't do because she couldn't drive or speak English. We later moved to Jackson, which meant I didn't have to commute to work anymore. But that still didn't lighten my load because it only meant I had to commute to Lansing instead to go to school.

Once I settled into a routine, I got used to this lifestyle. Although it was extremely difficult, I was able to make it work. But I won't say it didn't take a toll on me. Because of this schedule and the lack of sleep night after night, I wasn't sufficiently armed for the spiritual battle that would soon come my way.

NOTES

1. https://www.brainyquote.com/quotes/neale_donald_walsch_452086.
2. *Ice Castles,* Imdb.com, Imdb.com/title/tt0077716/characters/nm0000913?ref_=tt _cl_t1.

Chapter 4

Losing My Convictions

*Beware of false prophets, which come to you in sheep's
clothing, but inwardly they are ravening wolves.*

—Matthew 7:15

I remained active in the Church during my first two years of
law school. I was faithful in doing my home teaching and did
my best to magnify my callings as an elders quorum instructor
and executive secretary in the bishopric. I helped found the LDS
Student Association in my area and served as its first president.
I attended the Chicago Temple and lived close enough to visit
Carthage, Liberty Jail, Nauvoo, and Palmyra.

On my first visit to Palmyra, barely anyone was there. It wasn't
pageant season, so there weren't many tourists. At one point, I
found myself alone in the Sacred Grove. It was incredible standing where the Prophet Joseph once stood and where God and
Jesus Christ had visited him. I knelt in an opening and prayed. I
thanked Heavenly Father for everything. It was surreal praying
in the same grove where Joseph had prayed. When I finished, I
saw a small leaf on the ground in front of me. I picked it up and
placed it in my wallet. I carried that leaf with me until the day I
left the Church.

I will also never forget the feeling in Joseph's home and in the printing press where the Book of Mormon was printed. I felt as if I were on sacred ground.

Ironically, my last visit to Palmyra in my third year of law school triggered the events that killed my testimony. The last time I visited Palmyra was to attend the Hill Cumorah Pageant. If you've ever been to the pageant or other big Church events, you know how many anti-Mormons are there picketing. They're everywhere. As a law student, I believed I had the skills to debate with them and defend the Church. I wanted nothing more than to prove them wrong. I argued with them, and then I went home with a hunger to learn more about the gospel. My goal was to be the smartest member of the Church ever and be a great apologist for the Church.

I started studying the teachings of Brigham Young and other earlier prophets. I wanted to be as prepared as possible the next time I came across anti-Mormons. I didn't feel like I was able to get all of my answers from the scriptures alone, and I thought that reading other books about the Church would help. I soon realized that I hadn't been taught some of the things I was reading. I was surprised to learn about the Adam–God theory, polygamy, and some of the things Joseph Smith had done. I didn't understand any of these things. They didn't sound like they belonged to the church I knew and loved, and I began to wonder if this really was the true church. Would a loving God really allow some of these things to happen?

I felt alone in my confusion. I didn't have anyone to turn to for support. I was too busy to have many friends, I didn't have any family nearby, and the Hall family was hundreds of miles away. Communication thirty years ago was much different than it is now. We either had to write letters or pay large fees to call long distance.

I did present the bishop with my questions, but he basically told me, "Forget about those things. They aren't important." I don't blame him for saying that. That seemed to be the attitude of many of the leaders back in the eighties, and he was just trying to get me to focus on the basics.

But I felt like he was hiding something from me. If the Church didn't want to talk about certain things, I reasoned, then they must be ashamed of the past. Since I couldn't get my answers from my study materials or from the bishop, I turned to anti-Mormon literature, which was extremely open in discussing my concerns.

The more I read, the more I became disenchanted with the Church and saw it as a cult. I couldn't believe I hadn't been taught many of the things I was reading, and I couldn't believe that the true church could accept such things. On November 11, 1989, I woke up and realized I no longer had a testimony.

When I stopped attending church, some of the members told me I was going to hell for sinning against the Holy Ghost. Years later, my stake president said that wasn't true, but at the time I didn't know what to believe. But even if I was going to hell, I didn't care because I no longer believed in a Mormon god.

It took only about three months to transform from a completely active member of the Church to asking to have my name removed from its records. I had attended the Hill Cumorah Pageant in August, and in November I wrote to my stake president and asked to have my name removed. He sent me a letter saying I would need to attend a Church court (formally called a disciplinary council).

"Sorry," I wrote back. "I'm not going. I don't believe in your teachings anymore, and you don't have any authority over me anymore."

A few weeks later, I received a letter saying I had been excommunicated. (Back then, members who requested to have their names removed were automatically excommunicated.)

I was furious. I was furious that I had been deceived, that the church I once loved now seemed so corrupt. I was furious that I had almost lost my family and friends over my decision to be baptized and that I had spent eighteen months on a mission when I could've been progressing in my career or in law school. I was furious at the way the members had treated me and judged me, furious that I had been excommunicated when I had done nothing wrong.

Although many people become atheists after leaving the Church, I never lost my faith in God. The relationship I had developed with Him when I was a child could never be broken. Going to church was still important to me, but I no longer believed there was one true church.

I visited several different churches before finding the Church of the Nazarene. I attended church there for the next few months until I finished law school. When the members there found out I had once been a member of the Church, they asked me to teach some classes about it, and I happily obliged. I never sought opportunities to teach classes against the Church, but when people found out I had left the Church and asked me to talk about it, I seized the opportunity like a predator attacking its prey.

Even without the Church, I felt like I was leading a good life and things were still happening in my favor. By the time I graduated from law school, I had two children, a boy and a girl. I continued working for Judge Britten and even took on a second job teaching law classes to inmates in the prison through a community college program. Many of my peers spent weeks studying for the bar full time, but I didn't have that luxury. Just like before, I studied early in the morning or late at night.

When Judge Britten saw me studying before work, he would always say, "None of my clerks have ever flunked the bar." No pressure, right?

After I took the bar, I thought I was the first of Judge Britten's clerks to flunk it. I had given everything I had to finishing law school and taking the bar, but I had also given everything I had to my two jobs and to taking care of my family. My performance on the exam would be the true test of whether I had stretched myself too thin.

Graduating from law school.

I had to wait a painstaking four months to receive the results in the mail. If I passed, I would soon enter the Army, where I had been accepted pending passing the bar. All my life I had felt a duty to serve my country, and the time was finally right to join the military.

One day, around the time the bar results were due, my boss at the prison asked if I'd be returning the next school year to teach. I told him I had been accepted into the Army pending passing the bar and would let him know when I received the results. He explained that he needed to make the teaching schedule and asked if I could call home to see if my results had come.

I called my wife, and to my surprise the results had come in the mail that day. I tried to get her to describe the envelope to me. If I passed, it would be a thin envelope with a letter. If I didn't pass, it would be a thick envelope with the reapplication paperwork.

I couldn't remember the word for *thick* in Spanish, so I asked her if the envelope was *grande* (large). She said yes, and my heart sank. I knew I had flunked. I told her to go ahead and open the envelope, and she did her best to read me the letter. It sounded like she said "passed," but I didn't believe her. I called two different friends and asked if they could go to my house and read me the letter, but they were both unavailable. I hurried home to read the letter for myself.

The bar exam consisted of two parts—essay questions that were specific to practicing law in Michigan and multiple-choice questions that applied to practicing law in the United States. If I passed, I knew it would be because of my essay scores because I've never done well on multiple choice questions. I had been told that those who scored in the top 2 percent in the country in the multiple-choice questions would not have their essays graded; they would automatically pass the bar. I was positive that wouldn't be me. In fact, I was so certain I had failed the entire exam that I had written a letter to the principal at the school in Honduras where I had taught and asked for my old job back. I didn't want to retake the bar. It was too grueling and stressful, and if I failed I would be content teaching fourth grade again.

With trembling hands, I picked up the letter. I passed! Even more unbelievable, I had scored in the top 2 percent for the multiple-choice section. I didn't need my essays scores to save me.

I took the letter and ran to Judge Britten's office. I knocked on the door and said, "Your streak continues. None of your clerks have ever flunked the bar."

On June 1, 1990, Judge Britten swore me in as an attorney. Then I walked into his chambers, and LTC John Smith swore me in as a First Lieutenant in the US Army. I went to Virginia for three months for Judge Advocate General's Corps (JAG) school and then moved my family to Panama for my first assignment. I had been given a

*In June 1990, Judge Gordon Britten, the judge I worked for
while I was in law school, swore me in as an attorney. Afterward,
LTC John Smith swore me in as a First Lieutenant. I always
wanted to be an attorney and an officer in the US military.*

choice of where I wanted to serve and could have gone almost any-
where in the world. I chose Panama so I could speak Spanish.

Soon I started attending the Crossroads Bible Church, a non-
denominational church. When I was asked to introduce myself,
I stood up and explained that I was new in Panama and had
once been a member of the Church and had served a mission in
Honduras. As I was sitting down, the minister asked, "Were you in
Honduras in 1986?"

"Yes," I said. "I had returned to Honduras after my mission. I
was teaching school while waiting for my wife's visa."

"Did you attend an embassy party one night?"

"Yes," I said. A fellow teacher at my school had a sister who
worked for the embassy, and he had invited me to a party where
I had played the guitar and sung a couple of songs I had written.

"I remember you," the minister said. "I turned to your friend
and told him that I'd love for you to come be a part of my church
and maybe even teach my youth. You just seemed like the kind of
guy who'd be good at that. Your friend said, 'Forget about it; he's a
Mormon.' But I prayed that you'd come, and now here you are in
Panama and no longer Mormon."

How cool is that! I thought.

I ended up being his youth director, and I taught classes against the Church when opportunities arose. There was a cruise ship that would dock periodically in Panama, and they had a ministry that would pass out information about their church and invite people to classes. When they found out I had been a member of the Church, they asked me to speak. I gave three lectures for them while I was in Panama and told them all about the Church and how evil I thought it was. They even videotaped my lectures to use at other locations.

A couple years later, I was transferred to Honduras. I chose to go there, even though that was the land of my mission. I still loved the country and my mission (even though I hated the Church), and I loved my job in Honduras. I served as the legal liaison between the military and the American Embassy in Honduras, and while I was stationed there I was nominated for the award of Best Young Attorney in the United States Military. Unfortunately, I didn't win the award, but being nominated was a huge honor.

While in Honduras, I attended another nondenominational church. Being back in Honduras sparked memories from my mission, but it didn't spark my testimony. I still had hostile feelings toward the Church and was sorry I had led people "astray" on my

One of my greatest joys and honors was putting
on the uniform and serving my country.

mission. I sought out the people I had taught and apologized for teaching them false doctrine. One family told me they had already gone inactive. The others simply thanked me. The people in Honduras are too well-mannered to argue. I was only able to find a fraction of the people I had taught, and I'm not sure if my apology changed anyone's mind about the Church. But at the time I thought I was doing what I could to right my wrongs.

I stayed in Honduras for a year. In 1993, I was up for another transfer and took a position in Oklahoma because it was the closest open position to my grandfather. It had been nine years since I'd lived in Texas, and with my grandpa's age and ailing health, I wanted to spend as much time with him as possible.

In Oklahoma, I discovered the internet and a whole new world full of chat boards. It became so easy to find people to argue with and bash the Church. I didn't even have to leave my house! All of these people were right there on my computer screen, and I could say whatever I wanted and release my feelings of rabid hatred for the Church. By now I was a seasoned attorney and could out-argue anyone.

When I left Honduras, the commander took my sign off my building and had everyone sign the back of it.

I joined several different chat boards over the years and always used the same vicious tactics to attack the Church. With unfailing devotion I ridiculed the members of the Church and told them how wrong they were for following a false prophet, worshiping a false god, and belonging to a false church. Little did I know that my participation on a particular chat board and my friendship with a man on that board would eventually lead me back to the Church.

Chapter 5

Mike the Missionary

*Isn't it amazing how God brings the right people into
your life at the right time. People who support, love
and pray for you, regardless of your circumstances.*[1]

—*Author Unknown*

After several years of tearing apart people on chat boards, I
met Mike, who eventually became a good friend. My story
wouldn't be complete without him, and I know that God prepared
him to help me. He never lost his testimony and never became
anti-Mormon, but he does have his own story of falling away from
the Church and returning. I know he was able to use those experiences to have empathy and help me return to the Church.

Mike grew up near Provo, Utah, and was semi-active in the
Church. He believed parts of it but didn't have a full-fledged testimony. He got married when he was nineteen, and after nine years
and two children, his wife asked for a divorce.

Mike was devastated. He couldn't imagine life without his wife.
At the time he was in real estate and couldn't stand being alone in
his office with his thoughts. He was a member of the Elk's Club, so
he went down to the lodge one day and played poker. It didn't take
long for him to realize that he wasn't thinking about his problems
when he played, and poker became his escape. He decided that if

he was going to continue playing, then he needed to become good at it. He didn't want to keep playing only to lose money. Mike studied up on poker and got so good at it that he was able to quit his job. For three years he was a professional gambler and was very successful by the world's standards. He had a lot of money, a nice house, and a nice car. And the best thing was, he didn't have to sit in an office all day and deal with his mental anguish.

But even with all of that, he realized he still wasn't happy. Poker helped him escape his problems for a while, but the sadness was always there. Around this time he met his current wife, Lynette, who was also a member of the Church but not active. He made it clear at the beginning of the relationship that he would never get married again. The first one had ended so traumatically that he couldn't bear the thought of enduring so much pain again. But she loved him enough to convince him that maybe this time his marriage would last.

When they accepted a neighbor's invitation to a ward softball game, they realized they felt comfortable with the ward members. Maybe it was time to give church another chance.

Mike and Lynnette Robertson

The next January, the Sunday School teacher challenged the class to read the Book of Mormon that year. He explained that if they would just read the lesson each week, by the end of the year they would have read the entire Book of Mormon. Mike decided this was a reasonable goal and accepted the challenge.

He opened the Book of Mormon and couldn't put it down. No longer gambling, Mike was running a pawnshop and had a lot of down time at work. He spent that time reading the scriptures. He quickly finished reading the Book of Mormon and decided to read it again. The second time he got much more out of it. The third time he finished it with a solid testimony and decided it was time to make some serious changes in his life.

After church one day, Mike asked his bishop if he could talk to him. They went into the bishop's office, and Mike confessed years of sin. He felt like Alma the Younger when he was "racked with eternal torment, for [his] soul was harrowed up to the greatest degree and racked with all [his] sins" (Alma 36:12). Soon Mike was overcome with the Spirit and had an indescribable experience. He felt instant relief, and just like Alma the Younger, he could "remember [his] pains no more" (Alma 36:19).

In the bishop's office that day, Mike felt closer to God than he had his entire life. He would never forget the sweet spirit that filled him. If that is what heaven feels like, he reasoned, he would do anything to get there.

All of this happened before I met Mike. He and his wife have now been active in the Church for more than thirty years. Mike's testimony is solid, and he seeks opportunities to share it and help others who are struggling.

That's partly why he joined the chat board where I met him, although he arrived at it by accident. A couple years before I joined the board, Mike was searching for information online about the Church so he could study more. He searched the term "Mormon beliefs" and saw a link for the board "What Do Mormons Really

Believe?" It seemed like what he was looking for, so he clicked on the link. It didn't take long to realize that this was a chat board created only a week earlier by an ex-Mormon who was now an anti-Mormon. The board was riddled with haters trying to steer people away from the Church. But there was also a good mix of active Latter-day Saints who wanted to defend the Church, as well as struggling Latter-day Saints who were seeking answers.

Mike wanted to defend the Church, so he started engaging in the conversations. People would ask questions he couldn't answer, so he would carefully research those topics and then thoughtfully write responses. He was thick-skinned and wasn't bothered by those who tried to attack his beliefs. He had a genuine desire to share the gospel. He hadn't served a mission when he was younger, and he felt this was his way of declaring his testimony to the world.

In 1999, I joined the board. When I saw the name of it, "What Do Mormons Really Believe?", I couldn't pass up the opportunity to let people know what they really believed. I got into horrible arguments with others on the board. When I met Mike, I tried to have knock-down-drag-outs with him. I thought he was as true-blue as a person can get and was blinded by his faith. I used my quick wit and litigating skills to debate him, but he was always respectful and genuine. I asked a lot of questions that were worded as questions, but they were really statements meant to contradict Church doctrine. Mike knew this, but he always considered these topics carefully and would take the same approach he had done with other members of the board. He would pray and ask the Holy Ghost to help him understand it. Then he would research the subject, write down a comprehensive answer, and respond. The difference between Mike's research and my research is that Mike sought answers from the Spirit.

Mike was kind to everyone on the board, even people like me who only wanted to attack the Church. He gained many friends, and a few years later when the moderator decided to leave the board, he turned it over to Mike. The moderator left to become a minister at another church, but his attitude toward the Church had softened immensely. I have no doubt that Mike was influential in that change, just as he was in mine.

Mike truly cared about the people on the board and had a gift for seeing each of them as a child of God, whether they were active in the Church or anti-Mormon. When he discovered that some of them lived near him, he would find ways to help them with their problems, even doing anonymous acts of kindness for them.

He showed that same Christlike love to me from the beginning when he didn't take offense to my verbal attacks and always responded with respect. I was rude to him in the beginning, but he was never rude to me. When he became moderator of the board, he would tell other members to be kind to me. They thought he was crazy because I was trying to cause so much contention. But that's just how Mike is.

In a sense, Mike killed me with his kindness. By 2005, I no longer hated the Church. I still believed with all my heart that it was wrong, but I no longer believed it was evil. I ended my quest to destroy it and stopped trying to "lawyer" Mike into denouncing his faith. My questions became real questions rather than feeble attempts to prove the Church was wrong. Mike and I became two friends with different beliefs who agreed to disagree.

When Mike noticed that I was softening, he started putting my name on the prayer roll in the temple.

"Don't pray for me," I'd tell him. "I'm never going to be LDS again."

But Mike knew something I didn't know and faithfully put my name in the temple for the next decade.

When Mike and Lynnette became active in the Church, they set a goal to go to every temple in the world. Back then there were only thirty-five temples, so it was a much more feasible goal than it would be now. In 2005 they still hadn't been to the Dallas Texas

Temple and decided it was time to go. Although Mike and I had communicated online for years and had spoken on the phone a few times, Mike wanted to meet in person. He didn't tell me this, but he felt that talking in person would help him to better understand me and how to help me.

Mike and Lynette flew to Dallas, and we met at my house for dinner on a Friday night. They planned to go to the temple the next day, and I told them I would show them where it was. We drove in separate cars, and they followed me to the temple.

I waited outside for two hours while they did a session. I could have left and returned to meet them after the session, but I didn't mind. I still had respect for the temple and actually felt a longing to be inside. I had only been in the temple a handful of times, but I never forgot the peace I felt there and what it was like to be in the celestial room. While I waited for Mike and Lynette, I enjoyed the beauty and the peace of the temple grounds. I struggled to know whether my longing to go inside was from the Spirit or if I was simply having good memories.

The next day, Mike and Lynette went to church, but I didn't go with them. I didn't learn until later that Mike told the branch president and missionaries about me and gave them my number. Nor did I know that for the next few years he would call them periodically and have them check up on me.

Mike and I have been friends for nearly twenty years now. The majority of those years were spent with me saying I'd never join the Church and with Mike saying he was praying for me. We've had dozens—maybe hundreds—of conversations in which Mike patiently explained the gospel to me and bore his testimony. When I was so contentious that I could have destroyed Mike's testimony, his steadfastness in the gospel and thick skin kept him safe. Mike, ever patient and kind, refused to be swayed and refused to be offended.

Mike never gave up on me. God never gave up on me. And I know that God sent Mike into my life to show me that.

Now that Mike and I live in the same state, we get to hang out occasionally. Here we are at the Utah Republican Convention in 2016.

NOTE

1. Toska, Renato, 2015. "Isn't It Amazing How God Brings the Right People into Your Life at the Right Time. People Who Support, Love and Pray for You, Regardless of Your Circumstances." AgapΩ, Blogger, June 9,2015, http://ilove -agapo.blogspot.com/2015/06/isnt-it-amazing-how-god-brings-right.html.

Chapter 6

Becoming Catholic

*God may not guide us in an obvious way because he wants
us to make decisions based on faith and character.[1]*

—*Dallas Willard*

In 1996, I left the Army and moved to a suburb of Dallas, Texas.
I bounced from church to church for a while and finally settled
in the Baptist church in my neighborhood in Lancaster. I loved
being the music leader and often sang solos, but I never felt like
I had found a church to call home until I became Catholic a few
years later.

In 2002, I felt a strong impression to visit my grandfather, who
was living in Austin. He had been ill, and the prompting to see him
was powerful. I packed up my family and drove the three hours to
Austin. I sat at his bedside for a long time just chatting with him.
Though his body was weak, his mind was still sharp. During the
conversation, I asked him, "You have had a long, great life. Do you
have any regrets?"

He thought for a moment and said, "I think my regret is that
none of my children or grandchildren followed me in the Catholic
Church."

We talked awhile longer, and then my family and I drove back
to Dallas. That was the last time I saw Daddy Roy. He was rushed

to the hospital the next day. Four days later, he was gone. My hero, my confidant, and my idol was gone.

This is my favorite picture of me with my mom and her dad one Christmas. I love the joy on all of our faces.

At the end of the week, I returned to Austin for his funeral. I arrived early and was sitting in my grandfather's parish watching baptisms when I heard a voice say, "You're home now."

I turned around but didn't see anyone. Peace washed over me, and I truly felt like I was home.

At the time I was serving on the city council in Lancaster, and I immediately called the mayor, who I knew was Catholic.

"I want to look into becoming Catholic," I told him.

Twenty years earlier, I had made a similar phone call to the stake president and had met with the missionaries and had gotten baptized. This time I called a friend and took the Catholic lessons and joined the Catholic Church. I was active in it for the next twelve years. Eventually I became a Eucharist Minister and a Lector. I absolutely loved being Catholic, and it became a part of me the same way the Church of Jesus Christ had years earlier.

Some people may wonder why God so clearly told me to join the Catholic Church. If The Church of Jesus Christ of Latter-day Saints is the true church, then wouldn't He direct me there instead?

I had already tried the Church of Jesus Christ and left. When I became Catholic, I wasn't willing to give the Church of Jesus Christ another chance. God knew that, but He also knew that I still wanted and needed religion. This is the church that I could accept at the time, and God knew that my participation in Catholicism would help me understand the need for one true church and eventually lead me back to The Church of Jesus Christ of Latter-day Saints.

Looking back, I can clearly see how my membership in the Church helped me return to The Church of Jesus Christ of Latter-day Saints. After I left the LDS Church, I didn't believe in one true church anymore. For more than a decade I church hopped, finding the good in each church but never truly quenching my thirst for truth. The more I studied the Bible as a Catholic, the more I was convinced that there was, indeed, only one true church. I narrowed it down to two: the Catholic Church or The Church of Jesus Christ of Latter-day Saints. If there was no apostasy, then the Catholic

My Catholic confirmation in 2002.

Church was true and all of the popes received their authority from Peter. If there was an apostasy, then there would be a need for a restoration, which would mean that Joseph Smith was a prophet and The Church of Jesus Christ of Latter-day Saints was the true church. From what I read in the Bible, I didn't believe the Apostasy actually had occurred and therefore believed the Catholic Church was the true church.

Here is my reasoning for that conclusion: When Jesus was on the earth, He established His church. He called twelve Apostles to help Him and gave them authority to run the Church and perform ordinances, such as baptism. We know this authority as the priesthood. When Jesus died, the Apostle Peter became the leader of the Church. He, along with the Apostles, used their priesthood authority to teach the gospel, perform ordinances, and serve missions. However, people were quickly turning to wickedness and persecuting and even martyring the Apostles. One by one, all of the Apostles were eventually killed. Did they pass on their priesthood authority to someone else, or did their priesthood authority die with them? This is where Catholics and Mormons start to disagree.

The Catholics claim that Peter passed on the priesthood and that it has been passed down to every pope since. That means that the pope today received his authority from the previous pope, who received it from the previous pope, and so on until the authority can be traced back to Peter, who received his authority from Christ himself.

Members of The Church of Jesus Christ of Latter-day Saints, on the other hand, believe there was an apostasy after Jesus died. When all of the Apostles died, the priesthood authority died with them. No one else on Earth had been ordained with the priesthood, and therefore nobody had the proper authority to perform ordinances. Christ's true church was no longer on the earth, and it had to be restored through Joseph Smith centuries later. Some of Jesus's Apostles, Peter, James, and John, returned to the earth to give Joseph Smith the Melchizedek Priesthood. Because Joseph received the priesthood from them, he can trace his authority back to Christ. Today all priesthood holders are able to trace their authority back to Joseph Smith and Peter, James, and John, and ultimately to Christ.

The Catholic Church and The Church of Jesus Christ of Latter-day Saints are the only two churches who claim to be able to trace their priesthood authority back to Christ. All other Christian churches broke off from the Catholic Church and did not take any of the authority with them. Although they all preach of Christ and have good intentions, none of them have the real priesthood authority. (I am in no way condemning any of these churches or the people who attend them. They are wonderful, good people, and I know that God loves them as much as anyone else. But I also know that there is only one church that holds the proper priesthood authority.)

These facts, along with my Bible study, helped me to realize that either the Catholic Church was true or The Church of Jesus Christ of Latter-day Saints was true. But I was convinced from my studies that the Apostasy never occurred, so I believed that the Catholic Church was the true church.

It felt wonderful to again be a part of what I believed to be Christ's true church. I loved everything about being Catholic—the traditions, the reverence, the candles, the prayers. I loved the beauty of the rosary and how it incorporates the scriptures. I loved the peace I felt when I walked into a Catholic parish and partook of the body of Christ through the Eucharist. To me everything about the Catholic Church was beautiful and sacred and filled a void in my soul.

Even today I still love the Catholic Church and have the utmost respect for it. I have wonderful memories of being Catholic and am extremely grateful for the years I was Catholic. But I know now that it was just a stepping stone in my life to lead me back to the true church.

Three years after joining the Catholic Church, I no longer hated The Church of Jesus Christ of Latter-day Saints. I still strongly believed that it was wrong, but my feelings toward it had softened tremendously. I was able to speak respectfully to its members and have discussions that weren't filled with contention. I still visited chat boards, but I didn't converse with people with intentions to attack them. I truly wanted to help the members of the Church see where they were wrong.

I owe part of that change of heart to the Catholic Church. Its teachings helped me to better understand where the members of the Church of Jesus Christ were coming from. When I narrowed down the true church to being either the Catholic Church or The Church of Jesus Christ of Latter-day Saints, I was able to see that the Church of Jesus Christ was just trying to do what the Catholic Church was doing. Both wanted to help people find Christ and receive the saving ordinances to return to Him.

However, my membership in the Catholic Church is not solely responsible for my change of heart. I also believe that Mike was instrumental in helping me change. His genuine friendship and constant prayers worked miracles. I've always believed that God answers prayers, but Mike's prayers for me over the years are another witness to me that God had not given up on me and was using Mike to prove it.

NOTE

1. Dallas Willard, doublequotes.net, http://www.doublequotes.net/quotes/faith
    -quotes-god-may-not-guide-us-in-an-obvious-way-because-he-wants-us-to
    -make-decisions-based-on-fa.

Chapter 7

Returning

*Pride is concerned with who is right. Humility
is concerned with what is right.*[1]

—*Ezra Taft Benson*

In 2009, the miracles started happening. I had to go down to the
Mexican border to do depositions. I had a client who could not
come back into the United States, so we had an agreement where
he would come to the border and go to the immigration office in
Laredo, Texas, and we would use the conference room to do the
deposition. Then he would go back to Mexico and I would go back
to Dallas. During that time, I contracted the swine flu, also known
as the H1N1 virus. It was a terrible pandemic that may have killed
200,000 people worldwide.[2] Because it was a new virus, doctors
didn't understand it and everyone was afraid of it. I couldn't find a
doctor who would see me.

I was on my deathbed. I can't say for sure that I was dying, but
it sure felt like it. I had to miss work, which never happens. I even
went to work with walking pneumonia once. But the swine flu was
powerful enough to knock me down.

I lay in bed for two or three days, sweating profusely from
a high fever and then getting chills because my body was shut-
ting down. My throat was sore, my sinuses were congested, I had

horrible headaches, and I felt like my whole body had been beaten with a baseball bat. I don't remember ever feeling so deathly ill.

During that time, there was a knock on the door. I was upstairs in bed, so my son answered it. To this day I'm not sure why he let the missionaries in and sent them up to my bedroom. I joke that I have since disowned him, but in reality he has one of the kindest hearts and would do anything to help someone. I'm sure he didn't want to offend the missionaries, and maybe the Spirit nudged him to invite them in, even if he didn't understand what was happening.

The missionaries' visit was short, and most of it is a blur since I was so sick. I can't even picture their faces. But I do remember being irritated that they were there. I was in no position to receive visitors, let alone missionaries from the church I wanted nothing to do with.

"You're sick," they said.

Boy, I thought, *missionaries have incredible senses of observation.*

"I'm not just sick," I told them. "I'm dying. Now please get out of my house."

"Can we at least give you a blessing first?" one of them asked.

It couldn't hurt. Doctors wouldn't see me, so I could at least try this. Even if I didn't believe in the missionaries' teachings anymore, I still believed in God.

"If it'll get you out of my house, then yes," I told them.

They gave me a blessing. I felt instant relief. I was immediately and completely healed. My fever broke, and I was able to get out of bed even though I wasn't able to just a few minutes before. I walked the missionaries downstairs and asked them to never come back. I was grateful they had healed me, but I still wanted nothing to do with them.

I was relieved to get them out of my house, yet their presence didn't entirely leave. I was left with a nagging feeling to read my mission journal, and I kept thinking about the Church. Was God trying to tell me something? Why did the missionaries just happen to knock on my door that day?

I found a new chat board and posted a thread called "I Am So Torn." I explained how I loved being Catholic but felt a pull toward The Church of Jesus Christ of Latter-day Saints. I ended up rationalizing everything by saying that I probably just had good memories from my mission. I really didn't want to be a member of the Church again. Then I left the board and completely forgot about ever being on the board.

I started reading my mission journal, and all of the wonderful feelings from that time returned. During the next few weeks I attended sacrament meeting a few times. The missionaries were teaching a family who spoke Spanish and asked if I would go with them to a discussion. They knew I had served a mission in Honduras and needed someone to interpret. I didn't want to go, but I also don't like to turn down opportunities to help people. I went to the appointment but didn't bear my testimony because I didn't have one. I simply translated for the family and told them the details of the discussion. When I left the appointment, I didn't feel any different than I had when I arrived. I hadn't had any spiritual experiences or a confirmation that the Church was true.

But I continued to seek answers and tried to gain a testimony. I read from the Book of Mormon and prayed. I even went to the temple and read the scriptures in the waiting area where people without recommends are allowed.

I made an appointment with the stake president and asked what it would take to get baptized again. He said I'd have to have a Church court.

"Court is for someone who has done something wrong," I told him. "I haven't done anything wrong. All I did was ask to have my name removed from Church records."

But that marked the end of the discussion and my thoughts about getting baptized. I didn't like the stake president's answer about needing a Church court, and I hadn't felt anything when I tried to regain my testimony. I reasoned that the Church must not be true and that I should remain Catholic.

Looking back, I know that I didn't receive answers to my prayers because I wasn't humble. In the Book of Mormon, Moroni tells us that we have to ask "with a sincere heart, with real intent" (Moroni 10:4). I didn't have either of those at the time. Curiosity, maybe. But I wasn't prepared to submit my will to God's and act upon any answers He may have given me. If I were humbly seeking an answer, I wouldn't have taken offense when the stake president said I would need a Church court. If I were truly humble, I would have done anything it took.

My first wife and I eventually divorced. She is a good person and the mother of my two biological children, but we weren't a good match. I didn't want to get divorced and leave like my dad did, but after trying for years to make things work, we decided we weren't meant to be.

Susan and I started dating in 2009, and we were married on April 1, 2010. We love to laugh and felt that April Fool's Day was an appropriate anniversary for us. But it's no joke how much I love her and how much her love for me has changed me. On that day in April, I started a new life—an incredible life—that I never dreamed possible. Susan is my rock and my best friend. She has supported me in every decision, encouraged me, and celebrated my successes with me. We are both busy with our careers and have spent a lot of time apart because of it, but we always make time for each other.

Susan was Baptist when we met but supported my Catholic faith and attended Mass with me when she could. She has always believed in God, and her faith gives me strength when mine is weak.

Soon after we were married, our house caught fire upstairs around the gas water heater. My first thought was to protect my wife and family. I sprinted down the stairs and told everyone to get out of the house. I gave orders for my daughter to call 911 and for the rest of the family to gather the six dogs and get out. I was sure the house would explode and told Susan to get as far away from it as possible. Then I ran back upstairs to put out the fire.

Susan followed me up the stairs, determined to be with me at all costs.

"Get out of the house," I told her.

She looked at me with the most incredible look of love I have ever seen. Her eyes seemed to say, "If we die, we die together."

We worked together getting water from the bathroom and throwing it on the fire. I kept expecting the house to explode. When the firemen arrived, we were putting out the last of it. The lead fireman told us we shouldn't have been in the house. He didn't know why it hadn't exploded.

But I know why it hadn't exploded. And I know God knows why it hadn't exploded.

Susan and I on our wedding day in 2010.

I'll never forget the look of love in Susan's eyes when she refused to leave me. In that moment I knew that I was the most important person in the world to her and that she would live and die for me. I'd never felt so loved by anyone.

Throughout my life God has looked at me with an even more powerful love. He sent His Son to live and die for me. No matter how many mistakes I've made in life, He still loves me and treats me as if I am the most important person in the world.

God showed that type of love for me when I was a child by giving me a loving mother and grandparents. He showed it to me again when I was twenty-three and found the Church, and then again when I decided to go on a mission. Even after I left the Church, He continued to bless me with good things in my life. And then He showed me His love by bringing Susan into my life.

It's not a coincidence that I was drawn to Susan. She is one of God's gifts to me and is the perfect companion for me. Because of her I have been able to let go of the past, live richly in the present, and look to the future with hope and anticipation.

From 2010 to 2014, I enjoyed being happily married and happily Catholic. I didn't spend as much time online anymore because I was enjoying life with my best friend. We started traveling together and went on road trips, visited New York City, and went on several cruises.

In 2014, my life started changing rapidly. Susan was offered a promotion as a district manager for the photography company she worked for. The only problem was that the job was in Baton Rouge, Louisiana. In my mind, "promotion" and "Louisiana" don't belong in the same sentence, but it was a good opportunity for her. I didn't want her to pass it up, even though it meant we would have to live in two different states. My life was in Texas. We had a nice house with a balcony and a front porch that we loved. More important, I had a successful career as a managing attorney and couldn't pick up and leave.

"Take the promotion," I told her. "It's your dream. If you want to do that, go do that. You can take the position until an opening comes up in Dallas, and then you can do a lateral transfer."

Susan took the promotion, and we met once a month in Shreveport, Louisiana, which was about halfway between Dallas and Baton Rouge. Of course, it was difficult being so far apart, but we had a mutual respect for each others' dreams and made the best of our situation. After all, it would just be temporary until she could return to Dallas and life could go on as normal.

It's funny how naive I was at the time. Life never did return to normal. Someone on the outside might say my life was turned upside down with all the changes, but in reality Heavenly Father was turning it right side up.

On a cruise with Susan.

By now I was having serious doubts that the Catholic Church was the true church. I absolutely loved being Catholic and loved the doctrine and Mass. But I started having doubts that the Pope was truly God's mouthpiece. And even though I loved the Catholic doctrine, I never felt the same camaraderie with the Catholics that I did with the members of the Church of Jesus Christ. Catholics show up for services and then go home. Of course they are nice people, and you can make friends at church, but he Catholic Church doesn't have the same programs that the Church does. When you're a member of the Church (or even when you're not), you can call up the bishop or another quorum leader and state a need that you have. Within minutes, fifteen different people might show up at your house to help. When I was Catholic, I missed that sense of belonging to a ward family.

After Susan moved to Louisiana, I had more free time, so I spent more time online and joined another chat board. Without realizing it, I joined the same chat board that I had left five years earlier after posting the thread "I Am So Torn." I didn't remember being on that board before, so I joined under a new name—CountryBoy. Someone named GardenGirl messaged me and said, "I feel very drawn to you. Can we communicate?"

I wrote back and said, "I don't mind doing that, but I must warn you that I'm married."

She said, "I'm seventy-five. Get over yourself."

We began messaging back and forth. She was a member of the Church and knew that I was not. I told her I would never be a member again, but I agreed to talk to her.

After we began talking, my post "I Am So Torn" from 2009 somehow got bumped up to the top of the page. I have no idea how someone found it after five years, but people on the board started talking about it and responding to it. I had posted that thread under a different username because in 2014 I didn't remember being on the same board. GardenGirl saw the post and asked if I had posted it.

One day she asked if we could talk on the phone.

"Let me ask you a question," she said. "Do you have anybody in your family in the LDS Church?" I still didn't know her real name.

"No, I do not." Then I said, "Hang on, I do. I don't know him. I've never met him. I've heard of him, but for all I know he's dead. His name is Dean Jessee." Dean Jessee is a Church historian and head of *The Joseph Smith Papers*.

There was a long pause.

"Dean Jessee is your cousin?" she asked.

"Yes."

"Dean Jessee is my cousin!"

This seventy-five-year-old woman is a cousin of mine I never knew existed. We share the same ancestor who came across into this country from Europe. What an amazing discovery! How was it possible that I found a cousin on this obscure board?

She felt drawn to me. It was not a coincidence.

In January 2015, Susan received a call from her supervisor. He had bad news. Again. Her district in Louisiana was closing. She was told she would soon receive paperwork to terminate her position with the company. A short time later, the vice-president of the company called her and said, "Don't sign anything. There's a similar position open in Baltimore. Put your paperwork in for that. There's about a two-week vetting process, but I'd like you to have that position."

Susan and I weighed our options and decided that this was the best move for her career. I wouldn't be able to visit her every month, but we talked about getting together every three months.

I called my friend Mike and said, "Please do me a favor. Please pray for Susan. We need her to get this job in Baltimore."

"Okay, I'll do that," Mike said. "I'll put your names in the temple."

And then I got really crafty. "However, Mike," I said, "if God really wants me to be LDS, He'll send Susan to Salt Lake instead."

There wasn't a position open in Salt Lake, and I knew that. I was just being clever and thought it was funny. I mean, there was no opening in Utah. At least not that day.

The next day, the person who had a similar position in Salt Lake retired. Susan's paperwork was transferred to Salt Lake instead of Baltimore. She was hired immediately without any vetting. I was stunned.

I called Mike. "You're not going to believe this. Susan's going to Utah."

I heard him chuckle.

"Well," he said, "you know what you told God."

"I was just kidding," I said, almost in protest.

"God wasn't," he stated matter-of-factly.

It was time for me to seriously consider what I believed and decide if I was willing to do whatever God asked. A year earlier, I would've remained adamant that I was Catholic and that the Catholic Church was the true church. But I didn't know that anymore. I also didn't know if The Church of Jesus Christ of Latter-day Saints was the true church, but it was time to hit my knees—this time with humility.

"Okay, Heavenly Father," I said, "if you want me to be LDS, then that's fine. But you're going to have to do some things because I have questions and issues that no one has ever been able to resolve. Of all the people I've talked to and debated over the years, no one has been able to answer my questions. They've had twenty-six years to do that."

Over the next weeks, the answers came. I'd wake up in the middle of the night with an answer—an answer I had never heard before but it worked for me.

I had been troubled by the lack of archaeological evidence of the Book of Mormon. We all know where the events in the Bible took place. Bethlehem, Jerusalem, and all the other biblical cities are clearly marked on every map. If I choose to, I can travel there and see the sites for myself. I can walk where Jesus walked.

No one knows for sure where the events of the Book of Mormon took place. There are many theories that it happened in Central and South America, and then there are some scholars who have presented evidence that it actually took place in North America, right here in the United States. But God has never given us a definitive answer. We can't look on a map and point to Zarahemla. Most people in the world haven't even heard of Zarahemla. Does that mean it never existed, that the events described in the Book of Mormon never happened? That's what I used to think.

Finally, God gave me an answer that made sense.

"If you walk the streets of Jerusalem," God asked me, "does that make the Bible true?"

"No," I said.

"But what if tomorrow an archeologist down in South America or somewhere found a sign and wiped it off and discovered that it was 'Zarahemla, population 450'? What would that do?"

"It would make the Book of Mormon absolutely true," I said.

"Well, then, where would be your faith?"

That was an answer I could accept. It was such a simple answer based on the first principle of the gospel, yet it finally made sense to me that with some things we just have to go by faith. We won't have answers to everything when we want them. Sometimes God just wants us to have faith.

I also had issues with Joseph Smith. Some of the things he did didn't seem like things a prophet would do. I didn't like the story (or is it just folklore?) of him being a treasure hunter. Why would God choose someone like him to be a prophet and restore the true church?

"Okay, Mr. Attorney," the Lord said. "Who would you have chosen? Would it have been you, who questions everything? Would a doctor—someone who always needs proof and evidence to fix something—have been more to your liking? Or how about my plan, where it's a person who's open to the suggestions that there's other stuff out there? Who would you have chosen, Mr. Attorney, since you're so smart?"

In that moment, I knew that I would've chosen Joseph Smith and that the Lord indeed had chosen him. Joseph Smith was humble and teachable. I had not been.

I hated that there were several different accounts of the First Vision. I understood the claims that Joseph related it differently to different audiences, but as a litigator that didn't sit well with me. When I'm in court and a witness changes his story, I immediately know that he's lying.

One day I was telling Susan the story of the First Vision. It wasn't the first time I had told it to someone that day. I figured she didn't need to know all the superfluous details, so I left them out. She kept interrupting me and asking questions.

I got frustrated that she kept asking so many questions. "I hate when people interrupt me," I told her.

She said, "If you would tell me everything, I wouldn't have to ask you so many questions."

I realized I was doing the same thing Joseph Smith was doing with his different accounts of the First Vision. I was telling people different things based on who they were and what I thought they already knew. It was a hard way to learn that lesson because Susan and I had argued, but it finally dawned on me that people tailor their stories to their audience. Sometimes they add details they feel are necessary. Other times they only need to relate a brief summary. It all depends on who the person is talking to, but the story is always the same, even if it's being told a little differently.

I've started doing that with my own story of conversion. I've spoken at dozens of firesides, and I always tell my story a little differently, based on what the Spirit tells me to say. I never use a prepared script but always speak from my heart. Sometimes I go into great detail about certain experiences; other times I don't mention them at all. But that doesn't mean all of these things didn't happen. And it doesn't mean that if I don't tell one audience a story, I was making it up for another audience.

I finally understand why Joseph Smith told different accounts of the First Vision. He wasn't lying or trying to hide anything by telling different versions. He was simply doing what I do: telling different versions, as prompted by the Spirit, to best touch the lives of those who are listening.

On the morning of March 16, 2015, I was on my knees praying, as I did every morning, and suddenly, I realized my testimony was back. In my mind I could see the Lord walking up to me with His hands cupped, holding something precious. He said, "Okay, I've had this for twenty-six years. I've kept it nice and safe for you. Now it's your turn to take care of it." In my mind, I saw the Lord place His hands over my heart and give me back my testimony.

And when it came back, it all came back. No longer did I think the Church was true except for this piece of doctrine or that piece of doctrine. The Spirit filled me with joy and knowledge that I didn't have before.

For the first time, it occurred to me that a testimony is a living, breathing thing. I always thought (when I was a member of the Church the first time) that your testimony was up in something like the iCloud. You'd walk up to give your testimony and you'd pull it down. Then you'd bear your testimony and put it back up in the cloud and sit down. But it's not like that. If you don't feed it and nurture it daily, your testimony will die.

Overwhelmed with the Spirit, I called Mike. "I just want you to know that the Church is true," I told him. "Joseph Smith was a true prophet." I finished bearing my testimony to him, and he bawled like a baby. He had always said I would return to the Church someday, but he didn't always know if it would be in this life or the next.

I then called Susan and said, "I'm getting rebaptized."

She said, "Whatever you want to do, I'll support you."

I called the bishop and told him I wanted to get baptized. I met with him and then with the stake president, the same man who had told me in 2009 that I needed to have a Church court in order to get rebaptized. Of course the policy hadn't changed, and I knew that, but this time I was ready to attend the Church court if that's what it took. I was willing to do anything to get baptized again. It's amazing how your motivation changes when you have a real testimony. The stake president could sense my change of heart and became my biggest advocate to help me get baptized.

In the meantime, I visited Susan in Salt Lake in April 2015. It was both Easter weekend and general conference weekend. I was on my morning five-mile walk and enjoying it—sort of. I would have enjoyed it more if I could breathe. The elevation change from Texas to Utah is brutal.

All of a sudden, the Lord said, "This is home now."

Shocked, I replied, "No, it's not. Texas is my home."

"This is home now."

"No," I said. "I live in Texas. I'm licensed to practice law in Texas. I have a home in Texas."

"This is home now," He said again.

I thought, *Susan is never going to move here permanently. Susan is a Texan. Susan wants to go back to Texas as soon as a position opens up.*

When I returned to the apartment Susan had rented, I broached the subject. "Let me ask you a question. How do you feel about Salt Lake?"

"I've been wondering about how to talk to you about this," she told me. "I don't want to leave."

When the Lord wants you somewhere, He wants you somewhere.

I returned to Texas, determined to find a Realtor and sell our house. It was a beautiful home in a historic neighborhood, and I thought it would sell quickly and easily.

But the Realtor had bad news. My house was built on a pier and beam foundation, which is not a good idea for houses in Texas. I could put a marble in the middle of the floor and take bets to see which direction it would roll.

"You're never going to sell this house," the Realtor said. "Number one, you're going to have to pay thousands of dollars to get it up to code because of the foundation issues. By the time you spend that kind of money, you won't get what the house is worth."

I was disappointed but not defeated. I called Susan and told her we couldn't sell the house but maybe we could rent it out. She thought that was a good idea.

The week after I got rebaptized, a man knocked on my door.

"I want to buy your house," he told me.

"I really appreciate that," I said, "but the house isn't for sale."

"I'd really like to buy it," he persisted.

"I understand," I said, "and I appreciate it more than you can imagine, but I don't have the money right now to fix the foundational issues and the other problems it has."

He looked at me. "I want to buy it as is," he said.

Now my heart was racing. "How much?" I asked.

He wrote a number on a piece of paper and handed it to me. It was more than the house was worth.

After he left, I immediately called Susan. "You're not going to believe this," I said and told her about the man's offer.

"When God wants you someplace," she said, "He really wants you someplace."

My bishop and stake president wanted me to get baptized before I moved to Utah. I met with them and took all the necessary steps. The last thing I needed to do was have my Church court. I wasn't angry anymore about the Church court. I accepted it as one of the steps of repentance, and I was willing to do anything to repent. And as much remorse I felt for my sins, I wasn't worried about the outcome of the Church court. My bishop and stake president knew everything I had done, but they were still rooting for me. More important, I knew that God was rooting for me as well. If He didn't want me back in His church, He wouldn't have brought me so far. He wouldn't have answered my many concerns or taken Susan to Salt Lake and told me that I needed to go there as well. God was directing my life, and He would also direct me in the Church court.

Contrary to what I had thought in 2009, the Church court ended up being a wonderful experience. My stake president directed the meeting and was my biggest supporter. I knew he loved me and understood my sincere desires. He wasn't there to point out everything I had done wrong but to acknowledge how much I had changed.

One of the men present asked, "What happens if you hear something you don't like again and leave the Church?"

"There's nothing that I haven't already heard," I said. "I've used all the old stuff against Mormons. But if there's something new that antis are using that I don't know about and have not used against Mormons for twenty-six years, please tell me now."

Everyone in the room laughed.

Then I added, "I'm a different person than I was in 1989. I was twenty-nine years old, going to law school, living off three hours of sleep a night, trying to work, trying to raise a family, trying to study for the bar. Now I'm almost fifty-five. I have people to support me now. I hope to be living in Salt Lake soon, where I'll have even more support. I didn't have support back then. None of the conditions that existed back in 1989 exist now. I'm a stronger person now. I'm not living on three hours of sleep. I have a support circle that I can go to now when I need strength."

I was asked to go into the stake president's office while the council made their decision. It did not take long. They called me back a few minutes later, and the stake president said, "We'd like to welcome you back into the Church."

I was truly humbled. I'll never forget how my stake president served as my advocate during that meeting. I felt as if he were my lawyer arguing in my behalf and proving that I had served my time. He reminded me of another advocate that I have—my Savior, Jesus Christ, who heard my prayers and pleaded His case in my behalf to the Father. Because of Him, I could have a second chance.

"When can I get baptized?" I asked, eager to get back to where I belonged.

"As soon as you want," the stake president said. "You can do it this evening if you want."

I couldn't get baptized that evening, but I knew I'd do it soon. As soon as the meeting was over, I went to my car and called Mike.

He was overjoyed. "I want to come out for it," he said. "I want to be the one to baptize you."

I would have loved for him to baptize me. It seemed appropriate after all he had been through with me. But my logic took over and I said, "No, please don't come. I don't want you to spend that kind of money flying out to Texas for just one weekend."

Mike respected my wishes and didn't come, but when I went to the Salt Lake Temple the first time since receiving the restoration of my blessings he was there. I couldn't ask for a better friend. I know God sent Mike into my life to bring me back to Him. Mike regrets not serving a mission when he was younger, but he has certainly served a different type of mission. I will always consider him my missionary.

Unlike the first time I got baptized in 1983, I didn't have opposition from my family and friends. Everyone was supportive and excited for me. I guess that's why Satan felt like he had to step in and try one last time to stop me.

One night I had a dream that I was walking the streets of Nauvoo. People were talking about a statue at the end of the road on the far side of town.

"Don't go near it," the people warned. "It's evil."

Haughtily I replied, "I can touch it. I'm not afraid."

I walked to the end of the street and touched the statue to prove that I could. A horrible sense of evil filled me. It seemed to be squeezing me and tormenting my soul.

Wake up! I shouted in my mind. Somehow I knew this was only a dream.

When I finally woke up, my Great Dane was standing over me, clearly trying to protect me. Susan was living in Utah, so I was alone in the bed with my dog standing over me, growling ferociously. The hair on his back and neck was standing straight up, and his eyes were focused intently on something on the wall. I'd never heard such a menacing growl from him, and I was afraid.

The evil presence from my dream was now in my room. The air was heavy and thick and seemed to be suffocating me. I still felt the presence squeezing me and trying to destroy me. All I could do was call out, "Help me! Help me!"

Seconds felt like hours. Finally the presence left. My dog relaxed and lay back down. A sense of peace overcame me, and everything returned to normal. If I had only found my dog standing over me when I woke up, I would've thought that he just sensed that I had a bad dream. But his growls and his hair standing straight up told me that I wasn't just imagining the evil presence. It was one of the most frightening experiences of my life.

Joseph Smith had a similar experience when he opened his mouth to pray in the Sacred Grove. I'm not trying to say I had the same experience; nor do I think I'll be called to be a prophet like he was. But I do know that good and evil both exist. When we set out to choose the right, especially when our choices will change the course of our lives, Satan does all he can to stop us. But good will always triumph over evil. God will always deliver us and thwart the adversary's efforts. We must always remember to call upon Him. He is always only a prayer away.

On May 23, 2015, I woke up early in Texas and called Susan in Utah. It was my baptism day.

"I wish I could be there," she told me.

"It's okay," I told her. "I know you can't. Besides, I don't want a lot of people there. It's the second time. No one needs to make a big fuss over it."

I got ready and drove to the church. Someone gave me my baptismal clothes and directed me where to change. Then I went to the Relief Society room and waited for the service to begin.

As I scanned the room, I saw the bishop, as well as my friend Steve Marsh, whom I had asked to baptize and confirm me. He is also an attorney and had served on opposing counsel on some of my cases. We had had some meaningful discussions about the Church, and he had helped me to understand some gospel topics in a new light.

I saw a few other ward members, but it was a small group, just as I wanted. And then I noticed McKay Judd, my friend of more than thirty years, who I didn't expect to see that day. McKay attended my first baptism in Austin. He was now living in the Dallas area, so I had invited him to my baptism and had originally asked him to confirm me a member of the Church and give me the Holy Ghost. He was serving as the bishop of his ward and had to decline, explaining that there was a ward activity he couldn't miss.

But the Lord intervened and brought him to my baptism. There had been a huge downpour the night before, and McKay had to cancel the outdoor activity. So here he was instead, and I immediately recognized it as a tender mercy.

I talked to Steve, and he agreed that McKay should confirm me. McKay was the only one who had been present at both of my baptisms. It was as if the Lord was using him to bridge the gap between my past and the present.

My baptism day in 2015. Stephen Marsh (left) baptized me, and McKay Judd (right) gave me the gift of the Holy Ghost.

My baptism day was simple. There wasn't a lot of fanfare or a party afterward, but it was exactly what I wanted. All I wanted was to be home again in the Church and to know that Heavenly Father welcomed me back.

―――――

At the beginning of July 2015, I moved to Salt Lake to be with Susan. I had no doubt it was the right thing to do. The Lord had definitely shown me that it was when my house sold. And the city gave me a spectacular welcome the day I arrived with a thirty-minute firework show. (Or maybe that was for the Fourth of July.) But I admit, I was still afraid. I didn't have a job yet, and even though I thought I could find one rather quickly, there was always the chance I wouldn't find one right away.

"You have to have faith," Mike would remind me. "Everything is in the Lord's hands."

I did have faith, but sometimes having faith means waiting. Sometimes we have to wait so long that we start questioning whether we understood the Lord's directions. But when we hold on, we will always see the blessings of our sacrifices.

That's exactly what happened when I moved to Utah. To my surprise, I didn't find a job right away. I didn't see a miracle like I did with the sale of my house. The Lord wanted me to be patient. And when I finally did find a job, it wasn't the job I wanted. It paid only a fraction of what I had made in Texas, but at least it was something. I took every opportunity I could to work overtime, sometimes working seventeen or eighteen hours a day. This continued for two years, and I began to wonder if I had made the right decision to move to Utah.

"This is where God wants us to be," Susan would remind me. I found strength in her unwavering faith.

Susan ended up leaving the job that had brought her to Utah. Her district closed, and her boss wanted her to accept a position in Houston. It was so tempting to go. If we moved back to Texas, Susan could continue working for a company she loved, and I could immediately find a job similar to the one I left behind in Dallas. On top of that, housing would be cheaper.

The best choices are often the hardest choices. Susan and I prayed about moving back to Texas, and we both received the same answer. We needed to be in Utah. We submitted our will to God's will, knowing that through these difficult times we would find the greatest joy.

Looking back, I can see why we were meant to stay in Utah. Since moving to Utah, I've had the opportunity to speak at dozens of firesides and share my story. I was featured in *LDS Living Magazine* and am now writing this book. When I was ordained a high priest, I was told that my story would be shared with the world. I feel like the Lord has given me a special calling to tell others how much He

Starting my new life with Susan in Utah.

loves them. I don't seek these opportunities. All of them have come to me. I never would have imagined that so many people would be interested in a country boy from Texas. But the Lord wants me to tell my story so that others will know that it's okay to struggle. It's okay to make mistakes. God still loves them and wants them back.

Susan and I both have jobs now that we love. We are seeing the blessings of our sacrifices. But our jobs are not the greatest blessings. The greatest blessings come from our experiences in sharing the gospel and the people we've met who have shared their own stories of how they are choosing to follow Jesus Christ.

*With Susan in Moab, Utah, exploring the
beauty of our new home state.*

Notes

1. As quoted in Spencer J. Condie, "A Mighty Change of Heart," *Ensign*, Nov. 1993.
2. Gholipour, Bahar, n.d, "2009 Swine-Flu Death Toll 10 Times Higher Than Thought," *Live Science*, https://www.livescience.com/41539-2009-swine-flu-death-toll-higher.html.

Chapter 8

A Special Witness of Christ

No matter where we are or where we have been,
we are not beyond the reach of the Savior.[1]

—*Gary B. Sabin*

Whenever someone gains a testimony, they start to recognize their sins and feel remorse. It happened to Paul in the New Testament, it happened to King Lamoni's father in the Book of Mormon, and it happened to me. I knew God wanted me back in the Church. The events leading up to my baptism were undeniably orchestrated by Him. But I still couldn't shake the guilt I felt for the twenty-six years I spent trying to destroy the Church.

Sometimes the steps for repentance are easy. If you steal something, then you return it or pay for it. If you lie to someone, you apologize and tell them the truth. But repenting isn't always so cut and dry. Some mistakes aren't so easy to fix.

I have no idea how many people I talked to over the twenty-six years that I was anti-Mormon. These people lived all over the world. I only saw some of those people once, and many of them I never met in person. I didn't even know many of their real names. I also had no idea how my words affected them. No one ever told me that because of me they were leaving the Church or would never join it. I didn't know if I had truly hurt anyone, and my actions haunted me.

When my bishop and stake president interviewed me for baptism, they asked me if I had a testimony of the Atonement. I told them I didn't deserve it. They didn't agree. As judges in Israel representing Jesus Christ, they could discern my change of heart and sincere desires. But still, the guilt continued to gnaw at me for more than a year.

In June 2016, I was at my stand-up desk at work when I got a phone call from a number I didn't recognize. I was job hunting at the time, and the number was local, so I answered the call, thinking it may be one of the companies I had sent my resume to.

"Will you please hold for President Uchtdorf?" a woman asked.

"Yes," I agreed, completely stunned. I had no idea what he wanted. I had had no contact with him previously, and I couldn't think of a single reason he would want to speak to me. Unless . . .

For a fleeting moment, I wondered if he was calling to tell me there had been a horrible mistake. Maybe I hadn't been worthy to get baptized after all. When I left the Church, some judgmental members had told me I had committed the unpardonable sin. Was it really possible that I had? Was he calling to tell me I couldn't be a member of the Church anymore?

Of course I was wrong. I'd had a Church court and had been found worthy to be baptized. But humans tend to have the "being sent to the principal's office" reaction when someone in authority wants to speak to them.

Soon I heard the familiar German accent that I had grown to love while listening to general conference.

"I hear you've returned to the Church after twenty-six years," President Uchtdorf said. "Will you please tell me about it?"

I gave him the short version of my story.

"Is that all of it?" he asked.

"No," I said, "but I figure you're a busy man. I gave you the condensed version of it."

"I want to hear the whole story."

I went back and filled in parts I had skipped. Still, he wanted to know more.

"Will you come visit me at my office?" he asked.

Of course I said yes.

His schedule didn't allow for me to go right away, so we met a couple months later at the end of the summer. We chatted more about my experiences and my return to the Church. I don't get nervous around people and wasn't nervous talking to him. However, I did feel truly humbled to be in the presence of an Apostle of the Lord.

At one point in our conversation, President Uchtdorf asked me if I had a testimony of the Atonement.

"That's a trick question," I told him. He seemed surprised by my answer. I continued, "I believe in it for you. I believe in it for everyone else. I don't believe in it for me," I said honestly. I hung my head and let the tears flow. "I've been horrible," I told him. "Absolutely horrible. I don't know how many people I may have led astray. I don't deserve the Atonement."

"Dusty," he said.

I looked up and saw love and kindness in his eyes. He smiled and said, "Your sins are forgiven."

More tears fell as an undeniable power washed over me. For the first time, I felt truly forgiven. The burden of my sins was lifted, and I felt the healing power of Christ's Atonement replace my shame and guilt with peace and joy.

In the New Testament, Mary is at the Savior's empty tomb on Easter morning, distraught that His body is gone. She sees a man who she thinks is a gardener and asks, "Where have they taken my Lord?"

The man says, "Mary," and she instantly recognizes Him as the Lord and falls at His feet.

When President Uchtdorf said my name and I looked up into his soft, loving eyes, I think I felt how Mary must've felt when Jesus said her name. In that moment Mary had felt the indescribable joy of being reunited with the Savior. In that moment I, too, felt the indescribable joy of being reunited with my Savior. President Uchtdorf was representing the Savior, and I finally knew that Jesus hadn't just died for the world, but He had died for *me*.

I left my burdens at the feet of the Savior that day and have never looked back. I still regret my actions when I was anti-Mormon, but I no longer carry the horrible guilt. I know the Lord has forgiven me and is pleased with my new path. And I believe that somehow the Atonement will make things right with anyone I may have hurt along the way. There are too many people to go back and apologize to. I don't even know how to find most of them. But I know that the Lord is merciful and will find a way to help those people. I know I did my best to repent and that Christ will make up the difference.

During my meeting with President Uchtdorf, he asked me if he could share my story in general conference. A few weeks later, he gave the talk "Learn from Alma and Amulek" in the priesthood session of the October 2016 conference. President Uchtdorf told the stories of Alma the Younger and Amulek from the Book of Mormon. Both men had turned away from their faith but later repented and became great instruments in God's hands. Then President Uchtdorf gave a modern-day example and recounted my story, calling me David instead of Dusty. After saying that my blessings had been restored and that I now take "every opportunity to speak to others about [my] transformation, to heal the damage [I] caused," President Uchtdorf closed with the following:

> There are many Amuleks in the Church today.
> Perhaps you know one. Perhaps you are one.
> Perhaps the Lord has been whispering to you, urging you to return. . . .

Our beloved Savior knows where you are. He knows your heart. He wants to rescue you. He will reach out to you. Just open your heart to Him. It is my hope that those who have strayed from the path of discipleship—even by a few degrees—will contemplate the goodness and grace of God, see with their hearts, learn from Alma and Amulek, and hear the life-changing words of the Savior: "Come, follow me."

I urge you to heed His call, for surely you will receive the harvest of heaven. The blessings of the Lord will rest upon you and your house.[2]

I have heard the life-changing words "Come, follow me." Even though it took decades, I heeded the call and have truly received

With Susan at general conference in 2016. Susan wasn't
a member of the Church yet, but she supported my faith
and attended meetings with me when she could.

"the harvest of heaven." I echo President Uchtdorf's invitation to follow the Savior. There is no greater blessing, no greater joy. I wholeheartedly believe that the "Savior knows where you are. He knows your heart. He wants to rescue you."

Let Him rescue you. Let Him heal your wounds and take upon Himself your burdens. Give up your pride and let Him carry you. There is no shame or weakness in doing so. It is when we go to Him with a broken heart that we find the greatest strength.

⁓

A month after general conference, my bishop decided it was time for me to be ordained a high priest. I wanted to share the news with President Uchtdorf and emailed his secretary. I asked her to please tell him and then explained that I would love to have him ordain me. I didn't know if it was inappropriate to ask him for such a thing and told her I understood if he could not do it, but it would mean the world to me if he could. I was ecstatic when I received the email saying he would love to do it.

On November 10, 2016, I went to President Uchtdorf's office again. He invited Susan, my bishop, and my stake president to attend the ordination. He asked us all to have a seat and said he wanted to chat for a bit before performing the ordination. I thought he was going to explain my new responsibilities to me or tell me what a joy it would be to have the higher priesthood. Instead, he spent thirty minutes talking to Susan.

Susan told him about her religious upbringing and her faith in God. At this point she had no desire to become a member of the Church.

"Bring what you have, and we'll add to it," President Uchtdorf told her. "I know Dusty wants to be sealed to you in the temple. We'll save a place for you there."

The next evening, Susan told me she was ready to take the discussions. She could not see my stunned look, nor could she feel my soaring heart and soul. We began the discussions. She asked thousands of questions. And she was baptized about ten months later. I emailed President Uchtdorf's secretary and asked her to thank him for being so instrumental in both of our lives. About a week later, we received a signed letter from President Uchtdorf, congratulating Susan on her baptism. That isn't the only time he has written to me personally. The same night that he spoke about me in general conference, I received an email from him, thanking me for letting him share my story. I was amazed by his thoughtfulness. I knew he had already had a busy day with three sessions of conference and that he would be conducting the session the next morning. I was touched that he would take the time to reach out to me personally.

President Uchtdorf truly cares about "the one." I am reminded of the parable of the good shepherd in the New Testament. The shepherd had a hundred sheep to care for. When he noticed that one was missing, he left the ninety-nine other sheep to find the one. It didn't matter that he still had ninety-nine sheep to care for. He wanted all of his sheep and went to great lengths to find the one.

President Uchtdorf is an excellent example of this. I am grateful for the way he has emulated the love of the Savior and has helped me to better understand how much the Savior loves me. There are billions of people in the world. The Lord could have easily still accomplished His purposes without me. But He came to find me and brought me back home.

I believe now that it is my duty to help others feel that love. I hope that somehow my story can help others recognize the Savior's love for them. When President Uchtdorf set me apart as a high priest, he said my story would be shared with many people and that I had an important work to do in the Church. I don't know everything that the Lord has in store for me, and I am not going to speculate. But for now, I know that He wants me to share my story. He wants me to tell people that He loves them and wants them to return to Him. Maybe in some small way I can help others return Home.

NOTES

1. Gary B. Sabin, "Stand Up Inside and Be All In," *Ensign*, May 2017.
2. Dieter F. Uchtdorf, "Learn from Alma and Amulek," *Ensign*, Nov. 2016.

Chapter 9

Susan's Conversion

You don't know everything, but you know enough.[1]

—*Neil L. Andersen*

Now that you know my conversion stories, I'd like to tell you about Susan's. Prior to our experience with President Uchtdorf, I never wanted to push religion on Susan. I appreciated how respectful she was of me and how she would attend church and ward activities with me even though she was Baptist. I wanted to offer her the same respect by not pressuring her to become a member of the Church. But after a while, I started teasing her.

"You know," I'd tell her periodically, "my patriarchal blessing says that I'm going to be sealed to someone in the temple someday. I'd sure like it to be you."

We'd both laugh, and that would be about the extent of that conversation. But we did have other conversations about the Church in general. Susan wants to know everything, not just about religion but about everything. She asks everyone she meets a lot of questions, and what she can't learn from the people she talks to she will research on her own. Because the Church was such a big part of my life, she wanted to understand it better. We would have a lot of gospel discussions, but it was mainly for her to glean information. Susan also learned about the Church from some of her coworkers, but she never had an opinion about it one way or the other. Even when she knew I was arguing with people about the Church, she didn't seem to have any hard feelings against it. (Although I was no longer anti-Mormon when I married Susan, I still debated with plenty of people on chat boards.)

Susan was Baptist and was always going to be Baptist. When she was a child, her mom would drag all of the kids to church every Sunday, but when it was their choice to go, they still went. Susan attended a Baptist college and has always considered herself very conservative, even more so than some members of the Church.

When she was transferred to Salt Lake City in 2015, Susan didn't think much of the fact that she'd be surrounded by members of the Church. She figured that if anyone tried to convert her, she would just decline any invitations to church and try to avoid the

With Susan at Snowbird Ski Resort. The majestic mountains are one of the reasons Susan fell in love with Utah so quickly.

subject. Besides, she didn't think she would make many friends or become close to anyone in Utah. She had no intentions of having an active social life. She was there to work. In Louisiana she had worked sixty or seventy hours a week, and she planned on doing the same in Utah.

Mike was excited that Susan was moving to Utah and wanted to do anything to help. At first he suggested that she move to Provo so he and his wife could befriend her and fellowship her. Susan said Provo was too far away from her job, so he then suggested she move to West Jordan, where his daughter lived. Mike wanted Susan to be near people who cared about her, but Susan wanted to live in a place that would best allow her to do her job. Mike was disappointed when Susan leased an apartment in the north end of Salt Lake. But as the months passed and certain events began to unfold, Mike told me he realized that God was in control and Susan was exactly where she needed to be.

Susan was at her new apartment less than an hour when the bishop called. He introduced himself and then said, "Your friend Mike told me that your moving truck won't arrive for another week. The members of my ward have some things you can borrow until your stuff arrives."

The bishop offered her a desk, a chair, a futon, and some other household items. Susan was blown away by their generosity. In Texas we barely knew our neighbors. We would say hi to the couple who lived on one side of us, but we never chatted with them for more than about twenty seconds. We never met the neighbors on the other side of us. Susan was not used to this type of friendliness, at least not in a big city. She grew up with Southern hospitality in her small hometown in Oklahoma, but it had been years since she had experienced it. She was overwhelmed that complete strangers would offer to lend her their belongings when they didn't even know if she'd take care of them.

The other big surprise that Utah offered Susan was the mountains. Even three years later, she is still in awe of the huge, majestic mountains. Susan fell in love with Utah immediately and decided she didn't want to leave. Even though she had insisted she wouldn't have a social life here, she quickly grew to love the people too. However, she didn't want to tell me that. She knew I was a true blue Texan and that I wanted to spend the rest of my life there. She was too considerate of my feelings to tell me how much she loved Utah. And she knew this assignment would only be temporary. Her company realigned district boundaries or closed districts every two or three years, so it was only a matter of time before she'd return to Texas or move wherever her company had a position for her. This wasn't a permanent relocation but rather an extended business trip.

Susan enjoying the Utah mountains.

Susan had been in Salt Lake a little less than a month when I visited her and the Lord told me to move there. Even with her intentions to eventually leave and I having no prior thoughts to moving to Salt Lake, we decided to make it home. It's amazing what happens when you stop questioning what you want and decide to go wherever the Lord takes you.

If we hadn't settled in Utah, we probably wouldn't have had the wonderful opportunity of meeting President Uchtdorf. Some may argue that you don't have to meet an Apostle in person to have a rich, fulfilling life and follow the commandments. However, I believe that our experiences with President Uchtdorf were instrumental in molding us into the people the Lord wanted us to become. His counsel changed us in ways that nothing else could.

"Bring what you have, and we'll add to it," President Uchtdorf had told Susan.

For the first time, Susan realized that if she became a member of the Church, she didn't have to turn her back on her Baptist upbringing or the truths she'd learned as a child. The Church would not take anything away from who she was or what she believed. It would simply add to and complement what she already had.

That was a big moment for Susan. She had always thought that becoming a member of the Church would be a complete lifestyle change. Switching from Baptist to Methodist wouldn't have been such a big change, but she had always thought that joining The Church of Jesus Christ of Latter-day Saints would completely change who she was.

The night after she met President Uchtdorf, Susan came home from work with a migraine and went to the bedroom to lie down. I left her alone to rest but went in to check on her about an hour later.

"I'm ready to take the discussions," she told me.

But weeks later she asked, "Did I really say that?" She hadn't even been thinking taking the discussions. She just blurted it out when I walked into the room, which is out of character for this woman who has to learn all of the facts before making an educated decision.

The holidays were approaching, which was Susan's busiest time of the year at work, so she didn't begin taking the discussions for a few months. In the meantime, she attended church with me when she could and asked me a lot of questions about the gospel.

In March, she started the discussions. I don't feel like the missionaries were ready for Susan and all of her deep questions. The bishop and his wife attended all of the discussions, and the bishop helped with questions that the missionaries couldn't answer.

As I said, Susan wants to know everything. And she wanted to know everything before making a decision to be baptized. She read the Book of Mormon and prayed, and we had countless conversations. When she started reading the Book of Mormon, she realized there was no way Joseph Smith could have written it at his age and with his level of education. She knows a lot of intellectuals and realized that not even they would be able to write it.

Gradually Susan developed a testimony. She hadn't read the entire Book of Mormon and still didn't know everything, but she realized she didn't have to know everything. Even when she was attending the Baptist church year after year, she still had questions. She realized if she got baptized, she would continue to have questions, and that was okay. She knew enough to know that the Church was true.

One day she looked at me and said, "You know, I don't know what I'm waiting on to get baptized."

"Okay," I said, not wanting to waste any time. "Let's set it up."

I pulled out my calendar and looked at some dates. I ruled out a couple that wouldn't work and then said, "How about September 23?" I think she panicked and immediately regretted uttering those words, but we both knew she was ready.

Baptizing Susan was one of the best days of my life.

Susan's baptism day was incredible. Mike and his wife, Lynette, came, as well as the missionary who gave me the blessing when I had the swine flu. (I'll tell you later how I came into contact with him again.) We were overwhelmed with how many people from our ward came. Susan didn't know many of them personally, but they still wanted to support her. These were the same people who had tried to furnish her apartment when she moved to Utah, and they only knew her as a friend of a man who had called their bishop. This was the type of camaraderie I missed when I was Catholic—people showing up almost out of nowhere to help and support people they barely know, simply because that's what the Savior would do.

Baptizing Susan was one of the greatest privileges of my life. Not many men get to baptize their wife, and I feel extremely blessed to have had that honor. I'll always remember the smile on Susan's face when she came out of the water and the way she threw her arms around me.

We were companions before, but we became companions in Christ. I felt like I was home again when I got baptized, but those feelings were even stronger when Susan got baptized. Now I had my best friend and my wife by my side.

Susan and I thought we had a good life in Texas. Our life now is immeasurably better, even though we never thought we'd settle in Utah or that we'd both be members of the Church. "If you don't try to drive the bus," Susan said, "and just be open and willing to listen and go wherever you're supposed to go and do what you're supposed to do, it's amazing what can happen for you. In the past I always tried to be in charge of my own destiny. And so giving up the reins a little bit was really difficult for me. But it's been a huge blessing, and I'm not as nearly as tired from trying to make my own decisions."

Giving up the reins can be difficult, but sometimes it is by giving up the reins that we find our greatest freedom. If we don't, we miss out on the wonderful journey Heavenly Father has in store for us. Oh, what a journey it has been!

NOTE

1. Neil L. Andersen, "You Know Enough," *Ensign*, Nov. 2008, https://www.lds.org/general-conference/2008/10/you-know-enough.

PART II

Nurturing Your Testimony

As I stated earlier, when I regained my testimony, I had an epiphany. A testimony is a living, breathing thing, and if you don't nurture it, it'll die. That may be obvious to some people, but it wasn't always obvious to me. I used to think that once it was created, a testimony would always be there, kind of like a book. Once you write a book, your words are permanent. You can put a book on a shelf and not touch it for years. When you decide to read it again, the words are still the same.

It doesn't work that way with a testimony. A testimony is like a tender plant. It can live forever with the proper care, or it can wither and die quickly if neglected. Since 2015, I have nurtured my testimony daily with prayer, scripture study, and listening to promptings from the Holy Ghost. I have also taken every opportunity to share my testimony, which is one of the best ways to strengthen it. President Dallin H. Oaks said, "We gain or strengthen a testimony by bearing it. Someone even suggested that some testimonies are better gained on the feet bearing them than on the knees praying for them."[1]

In the following chapters, I will cover some of the common gospel topics that I have discussed with people over the years and will give you some tips on what to do if you have doubts. I hope my experiences will open your eyes to the truths of the gospel and help you develop, or strengthen, your own testimony.

NOTE

1. Dallin Oaks, "Testimony," *Ensign*, May 2008, https://www.lds.org/general -conference/2008/04/testimony.

Chapter 10

Why We Need a Prophet

*The teachings of prophets and apostles, past and present,
are as relevant to your life today as they ever have been.*[1]

—M. Russell Ballard

In 2015 we discovered that one of our sons has a severe form of dyslexia. It's not very common, and I had never heard of this kind. My son only understands words that have pictures, such as *car*, *tree*, and *house*. If the word doesn't have a picture, he can't understand it. He doesn't even see words such as *like*, *be*, *there*, or *it*. We would tell him things not knowing he was dyslexic, and he would only understand part of what we said. He would guess the rest, and many times he would guess wrong.

I believe that the world has "Religious Dyslexia." The world only knows part of the truth and guesses the rest. Many times they get it wrong. It's not their fault, just as it's not my son's fault that he has this disability. This is why we have thousands of religious denominations all teaching something different using the same book. They don't have all of the tools and the information that they need and are "only kept from the truth because they know not where to find it" (D&C 123:12).

As members of the Church, we have the right tools and know where to find the truth. Heavenly Father has given us the cure for Religious Dyslexia. We have a prophet who can interpret the scriptures and fill in the blanks. The prophet receives continuing revelation and knows exactly how to help us in our day.

No other church has a prophet. Many churches teach that there's no need for a prophet. God gave us the prophets of old, they reason, and everything we need is in the Bible. They claim there's no need for continuing revelation. But did God really stop speaking to us two thousand years ago? Would He really leave us to figure out everything we need to know with only one book?

I have a friend who said, "How can you believe there's a prophet?"

I said, "How can you believe there's not one?"

"We can't have one," he said.

This was my reply: "You have three kids, right? Do this for me. When those kids turn eighteen, I want you to take them into your office and tell them you're never going to talk to them again. Tell them, 'Everything you ever need to know I've already taught you or I've written it down. I've written it all down, so I'm never going to talk to you again. If you have a problem in the future, just go back to the things that you remember me doing or saying.'"

He said, "I can't do that."

I said, "So you're saying you're a better father than Heavenly Father?"

He said, "I didn't say that!"

I said, "Sure you did, because that's what you believe God did—gave us the Bible and then no more prophets after that. You think everything we need to know is in that Bible. That's all we need to know."

Did you know there are over forty thousand different denominations in the United States?[2] How are we supposed to discern truth with forty thousand different versions?

The answer is simple. We need a prophet.

The Old Testament prophet Amos taught, "Surely the Lord God will do nothing, but he revealeth his secret unto his servants the prophets" (Amos 3:7). God has called prophets since the beginning of time to teach us and to warn us. He didn't flood the Earth without any warning, but called Noah to preach repentance. Similarly, the Book of Mormon prophet Lehi preached repentance to his people before Jerusalem was destroyed. Isaiah and John the Baptist are among some of the prophets who taught of Christ's coming. Every time God does something, He first tells the prophet, who then tells the people.

We are not meant to walk alone in darkness during this life. God loves us so much that He has given us a prophet to shine His light on the path that will lead us back to Him. The prophet's words are simple and direct, and easy to follow if we will have faith.

In Doctrine and Covenants 1:38 the Lord said, "Whether by mine own voice or by the voice of my servants, it is the same." The prophet's voice is the Lord's voice. The prophet doesn't make up arbitrary rules to make us follow him. He teaches us and counsels us and explains the commandments to lead us back to Jesus Christ.

There has been no other time in history when we have needed a prophet more. Our world is full of violence, poverty, political unrest, and confusion. Can you imagine what it would be like without a prophet? Can you imagine the chaos that would ensue? What kind of loving God would not give us a prophet?

Our modern-day prophets have taught us how to get through these hard times by teaching charity, service, kindness, scripture study, and faith. We are tremendously blessed to have a living prophet today.

You may wonder, how can I know he is really God's prophet? How can I know he has really been called of God?

You can find out the same way you find out anything else is true: pray. I promise you, just as all of the prophets have promised, that if you pray with a sincere heart, the Spirit will bear witness to you that the prophet is indeed called of God.

Keep in mind that becoming a prophet does not make a man perfect. The prophet is still human, just like you and me, and still makes mistakes. He makes far fewer mistakes than we do, but he is still learning and improving just like the rest of us. The difference between a prophet and the rest of us is that he has a sacred calling from God.

Many people criticize the prophet and say surely God wouldn't call an imperfect man to be the prophet. But when has there ever been a perfect man on earth, except Jesus Christ?

Some people struggle with some of Joseph Smith's actions, especially with polygamy. Ever since my story came out in *LDS Living Magazine*, I've received about a thousand emails and Facebook messages. The number one question I get is "What are your feelings on polygamy?"

My answer is simple. I don't care. That's it. There are two possible answers to why polygamy occurred in the early Church: Either it's from God or it's not from God. There are the only two options. If it's from God, then that's way above my pay grade to argue with. Who am I to argue if it's from God? It is what it is.

If it's not from God, then it's a mistake. Now, before you think I am saying polygamy is a mistake, relax. I am not saying that. I am only saying that *if* it is not from God, then, by definition, it is a mistake. If it is a mistake, does that mean that Joseph Smith was not a prophet? If I walk into a courtroom and make a mistake, does that mean I'm no longer an attorney? Of course not. If a doctor misdiagnoses a patient, does that mean he's no longer a doctor? No. He made a mistake. Of course he's still a doctor. And of course, *if* polygamy was a mistake, Joseph was still a prophet. Disobeying does not make a prophet less than what he was called to be. It simply means he needs to repent.

When you get wrapped around the axle about an issue, go back to the beginning. Go back to the basics. Did Joseph Smith have a vision in the Sacred Grove? If he did, then he was a prophet. Bottom line. And if he did anything after that that you don't like, who cares? He's still a prophet. He is just a man. He made mistakes.

If we had as much day-to-day information about Moses as we do about Joseph Smith, we would find things about Moses we do not like or that we disagree with. But all we know about Moses is in the first five books of the Bible. And guess who wrote those? Moses.

You're going to see prophets in our day who do things that we don't always agree with. But they're still prophets. If the prophet says something in general conference or presents a new Church policy that you don't agree with, you should pray and ask God to help you understand it. If you have a confirmation that this man is a prophet, then you will also receive a confirmation that the prophet is speaking for God.

When I was thinking about returning to the Church, I read Elder Uchtdorf's talk "Come, Join with Us." That talk had a great impact on me, and I love what he said about the imperfections of the members of the Church and even the leaders of the Church:

> There have been times when members or leaders in the Church have simply made mistakes. There may have been things said or done that were not in harmony with our values, principles, or doctrine.
>
> I suppose the Church would be perfect only if it were run by perfect beings. God is perfect, and His doctrine is pure. But He works through us—His imperfect children—and imperfect people make mistakes. . . .
>
> It is unfortunate that some have stumbled because of mistakes made by men. But in spite of this, the eternal truth of the restored gospel found in The Church of Jesus Christ of Latter-day Saints is not tarnished, diminished, or destroyed.
>
> As an Apostle of the Lord Jesus Christ and as one who has seen firsthand the councils and workings of this Church, I bear

solemn witness that no decision of significance affecting this Church or its members is ever made without earnestly seeking the inspiration, guidance, and approbation of our Eternal Father. This is the Church of Jesus Christ. God will not allow His Church to drift from its appointed course or fail to fulfill its divine destiny.[3]

The prophet will never lead us astray. God will not allow it. Still, we live in a time when, more than ever, members of the Church are questioning the prophet. Over the past several years, many members have been upset about certain Church policies and doctrine that are not changing to fit the world's standards. Some people have even left the Church because they don't agree with the prophet's teachings.

If you are one of these people questioning, go back to the basics. Do you believe that the prophet was called of God? It's okay to have questions, but don't make things more complicated than they need to be. People often feel like they need complicated answers, but the gospel is simple. The pattern to receive truth is simple: pray with a sincere heart, ask God, and let the Holy Ghost speak to you.

I know that we have a living prophet who leads this church. I know that he speaks to the Lord and speaks for the Lord. He may not be perfect, but the gospel he teaches is perfect. If we humble ourselves and follow his counsel, we will be blessed more than we could have ever imagined.

NOTES

1. M. Russell Ballard, "Learning the Lessons of the Past," *Ensign*, May 2009.
2. Mary Fairchild, "How Many Christians Live in the World Today?" Thought Co., December 19, 2017, https://www.thoughtco.com/christianity-statistics-700533.
3. Dieter F. Uchtdorf, "Come, Join with Us," *Ensign*, Nov. 2013.

Chapter 11

No Coincidences

He knows your name and He knows your need.[1]

—Jeffrey R. Holland

I have seen God's hand in my life more times than I can count, and I know He isn't done guiding me. When we are humble and submit our will to His, having faith that He will lead us down the right path, God leads us to the right place at the right time. None of the miracles I've experienced have been as grand as Jesus turning water into wine or feeding the five thousand, but I still consider them miracles because I know that God was orchestrating certain events. This is especially true the year before and the year after I was baptized. Here are a few examples.

The quick sale of our house in Texas was certainly a miracle. About a year after we sold it, we learned even more about the divine events concerning it. Susan and I were at home in our apartment in Salt Lake. I got a phone call from a man who wanted to ask about our house in Dallas.

"I've already sold that house," I told him.

"Are you sure?" he asked.

"Pretty sure. I was there."

"Hang on a second." He started shuffling through some papers and said, "Huh. The guy who bought your house disappeared. Your house is in foreclosure. It's abandoned."

The man had given us the money for our house and then disappeared. I don't know if he even ever lived in the house. No one knows where he went or why he left, but he showed up on my doorstep and offered to buy my house at the exact time I needed to sell it.

On April Fool's Day in 2016, Susan and I were in Moab, Utah, to see the Delicate Arch and some of the other sites. We were in our hotel, and I was waiting for her to get ready when my phone rang. It was a sister missionary from the MTC.

"I see that you have just been on Mormon.org and want information on the LDS Church," she said.

I said "No, I was never on Mormon.org and I don't need any information." It was April 1, so I was sure this had to be a joke.

"Are you sure?"

"I have not been on Mormon.org."

Again she asked, "Are you sure? The only way I can have your information pop up on my screen is if you've been on Mormon.org."

I said, "I have not been there."

She said, "You have to have been."

I said, "I have not been. My computer is in Salt Lake City, and I'm in Moab at a hotel."

She said, "Well, do you want information about the Church?"

I said, "Let me tell you a story." I proceeded to tell her how I'd come back to the Church and how some of these miracles had happened.

She began to cry and said, "I'm at the MTC. I'm having a crisis of faith and they put me answering phones and responding to these Mormon.org inquiries. After hearing your story, I'm going to finish my mission." I hung up the phone in awe. What had just happened? How had it happened? The Lord is always in control.

After a fireside I gave in Ogden, Utah, a missionary came up to me with tears in her eyes.

"I've been struggling a lot," she told me. "I've thought about going home. But after hearing your story, I'm going to give my mission another chance."

I didn't inspire this young sister to stay on her mission. The Spirit spoke to her and gave her the witness that she needed. But God did put both of us in the right place at the right time so that our interactions could help God fulfill a specific purpose.

This happens a lot. Our paths cross with thousands of people throughout our lives. Many times the crossing of our paths seems insignificant, but we know that by small and simple things great things come to pass (see Alma 37:6).

In October 2016 my path crossed with two men while I was walking around Temple Square. It was the day after President Uchtdorf spoke about me in the priesthood session of general conference. I overheard a conversation between an older man and a younger man, who I assumed were father and son.

"You heard President Uchtdorf's talk," the father said. "Anyone can come back to the Church, even if they've been gone for a long time. There's still hope; there's still prayer. It happens."

"How do we know he didn't just make that story up?" the younger man said. "I bet a lot of the stories in conference are made up to build our faith."

I interrupted them and said, "Excuse me. I'm the guy President Uchtdorf spoke about."

The young man was skeptical at first, so I pulled out my phone and showed him a picture of me with President Uchtdorf. The young man was in awe and said something like, "That's so cool!"

"Everything that President Uchtdorf said is true," I told him. "Anyone can come back to the Church. There's always hope."

Our conversation was brief, and I haven't seen those two men since. But again, I saw God's hand in this experience. Why did I happen to be there in that moment? Why were they having this conversation right as I was walking by? Because God loves that young man and was using divine design to tell him. There are no coincidences.

In 2017, Susan and I had a date night at a gun show. All of our stuff was in storage, and I wanted a holster. On the way there, I told Susan I was beginning to wonder if I had misread God and if we were really supposed to be in Utah.

We arrived at the gun show and found a booth selling holsters. One of the folks working the booth started talking to me. He realized I was from Texas and told me that he owned land in Texas. He asked me what I was doing in Utah, and I asked him if he had heard President Uchtdorf's talk in the last general conference. He said he had. I told him, "The guy he talked about is me. That is why I am in Utah."

"Really?" he asked. "That was you?"

"Yes."

"Can I talk to you for a minute?"

Susan and I walked with him to a quiet place in the conference center, and another guy followed us. I told my story. After I finished, the guy who followed us said, "You're from Dallas, right?"

"Yes," I said.

"Oak Cliff?"

"Yep."

He said, "You probably don't remember me, but in 2009 you had the swine flu and were given a blessing."

I stared at him. I had to pull my jaw off the floor. He and his companion had blessed me when I felt like I was on my deathbed. We talked at length and agreed to meet for dinner at a later date.

On the way home, Susan asked me, "How is your doubt now?"

Now a word about that former missionary who gave me a blessing. After his mission, he had gone inactive. Before general conference in October 2016, his bishop said, "I'm tired of your inactivity. Here's a ticket to the priesthood session. Go listen to it. "

He went to the priesthood session at the conference center and heard President Uchtdorf's talk. The Spirit touched him and he returned to church, not realizing that the man in the story was the same man he had given a blessing to in 2009.

There are no coincidences.

Many people marvel at the number of miracles I've seen.

"Why can't I see miracles like that?" they ask. "Why can't God be in my life like that?"

"You can," I tell them. "And He is. You just have to recognize Him."

The Lord loves all of us. He doesn't limit His love to the prophet or the bishop or those who don't seem to commit big sins. He loves all of us. He loves *you*. And those miracles happen to all of us. The difference is I see them. I recognize them.

In the Book of Mormon the Lord told Nephi, "I am a God of miracles; and I will show unto the world that I am the same yesterday, today, and forever; and I work not among the children of men save it be according to their faith" (2 Nephi 27:23). You need to have faith before you can see miracles. And once you do have faith, you need to be aware of what is happening around you so that you recognize certain events as miracles.

A miracle doesn't have to be as grand as the parting of the Red Sea or raising someone from the dead. Those are definitely miracles, but most of the miracles we experience are as simple as talking to the person sitting beside you in class and later marrying that person. It's as simple as feeling like you need to make a left turn instead of a right turn and discovering later that you avoided an accident. A miracle is any event in which God shows us His love, and He shows us His love every day.

Have you ever had a bad day and then received a call from a good friend? That was a miracle. Have you ever had a problem and opened up the scriptures to the exact verse you needed to read? That was a miracle. Have you ever felt like you shouldn't do something, so you didn't? That was a miracle, even if you still don't know why you weren't supposed to do it.

Some miracles result from what we see as inconveniences. A few years ago, I overslept one morning. I was already late for work when I discovered the freeway on-ramp was closed. Irritated, I turned around to take another freeway, only to discover that that freeway was also closed. After more backtracking and more detours I finally realized I had to go the really long way to work. I had needed to go down Highway 75 but ended up taking the loop around Dallas. I was not happy. Later I learned that a man had been drinking and was driving the wrong way on Highway 75. He ended up hitting someone and killing them. Had I not overslept that morning, and had I been on Highway 75 as I had intended, I could've been the one in the accident. Instantly my perspective changed, and I saw my horribly inconvenient morning as a huge blessing.

God is acutely aware of each of us and loves us more than we can comprehend. He knows exactly how to help you in the moment that you need it, and if you pay attention you will see His hand in your life. Most of the time God doesn't shout at us or whack us on the head to get our attention. He speaks to us quietly through the still, small voice of the Holy Ghost, and we have to quiet ourselves enough to hear.

At times we will not be aware of the miracles that happen to us. We don't always know why sometimes we choose to take a different route home, or why we feel a prompting to talk to someone. But I promise you, if you were able to see everything that God sees, you would see Him constantly protecting you, constantly putting you in the right place at the right time, constantly intervening to give you the best life possible. Some miracles may go unseen, but it doesn't mean they don't happen.

The fact that you are alive right now is a miracle. The prophet Mormon said, "Who shall say that it was not a miracle that by his word the heaven and the earth should be; and by the power of his word man was created of the dust of the earth?" (Mormon 9:17). You are a miracle. God has a purpose for you and wants you here on earth. You may not know how, but He has brought you where you are today and has organized the smallest details of your life in ways you'll never know. You may be thinking, "Why did God bring me to this point? Why am I suffering so much? Why am I doubting so much?" To that I say, hold on. Just hold on for one more day. Look around and see if God is there. God doesn't show up at our door to visit us. Rather, He sends us blessings and sends good people into our lives. What are some of the good things that have happened to you recently? Who are some of the people who love you and want to help you? If you still feel hopeless after answering these questions, step outside. Look up at the sky. The sun shining down on you is evidence that God is there and loves you. Even if the sky looks dreary and the day feels darker than usual, the sun is still there behind the clouds. And the Son is still there, with open arms, ready to carry you.

Sometimes it takes years for us to overcome our doubts, fears, and insecurities. It took me a quarter of a century to truly recognize what God wanted for me. I hope it doesn't take you that long. But it's okay if it does. God is patient. God is kind. He will wait for you, no matter how long it takes.

I was in a play when I was in high school called *A Company of Wayward Saints*. In one of the scenes I played a doctor. I was an old-timey doctor and went to someone's house to deliver a baby. I was with the husband on the front steps of the house waiting for the wife to have this baby and the husband said, "Shouldn't you be doing something?" My response was, "When God is ready, He'll let us know."

"Do you believe in God?" the father asked me.

My response is this: "That's a difficult question for a man of science to answer in these enlightened times. But I know this. I know that God believes in me."

God believes in you. Even when you don't. Even when your faith is shattered. Even when you turn your back on Him, He never gives up on you. And the miracles are there, happening every day. You just have to recognize them. When you do, you'll be amazed at how much God is directing your life and creating opportunities to give you the greatest happiness. Don't forget the counsel in Proverbs 3:5-6: "Trust in the Lord with all thine heart; and lean not unto thine own understanding. In all thy ways acknowledge him, and he shall direct thy paths."

NOTE

1. Jeffrey R. Holland, "This, the Greatest of All Dispensations," *Ensign*, July 2007.

Chapter 12

What If I Have Doubts?

Doubt not, but be believing.

—Mormon 9:27

I've talked to a lot of people who have had a crisis of faith. As I mentioned, some of them have told me that after hearing my story they are going to give their faith another chance. Sometimes hearing another person's testimony and feeling the Spirit confirm its truthfulness is all it takes. That's one of the reasons we're commanded to go to church each week and to have testimony meeting once a month. By bearing our testimonies, either formally or informally, we strengthen each other.

But sometimes that isn't enough. Sometimes we have nagging questions that don't seem to have any answers, like I did before I left the Church.

First of all, know that it's okay to have questions. None of us understand the gospel perfectly, and it's normal and healthy to have questions. Heavenly Father doesn't expect us to blindly follow the prophet but rather to study and pray about his words.

We often think of Nephi as the perfect example of faith and obedience. But did you realize that even he had questions and asked the Lord for confirmation? In the Book of Mormon we read about Lehi's vision to take his family in the wilderness before

Jerusalem is destroyed. It was a difficult time for his family. Even though we mostly read about Laman and Lemuel murmuring, we know that Nephi also struggled. In 1 Nephi 2:16 we read, "And it came to pass that I, Nephi, being exceedingly young, nevertheless being large in stature, and also having great desires to know of the mysteries of God, wherefore, I did cry unto the Lord; and behold he did visit me, and did soften my heart that I did believe all the words which had been spoken by my father; wherefore, I did not rebel against him like unto my brothers."

The difference between Nephi and his brothers is that Nephi was humble and prayed for understanding. He asked the Lord if his father was speaking for the Lord and if their family really should leave their home. The Spirit confirmed to him that his father's teachings were true, and Nephi was comforted. After that witness, he was able to follow his father in faith, knowing that he was really following the Lord.

If we ask for answers, God will give them to us. In the priesthood session of the October 2017 session of general conference, Elder David. F. Evans shared his experience of seeking answers:

> As a young man, I had many questions about the Church. Some of my questions were sincere. Others were not and reflected the doubts of others.
>
> I often discussed my questions with my mother. I am sure that she could sense that many of my questions were sincere and from my heart. I think she was a little disappointed in those questions that were less sincere and more argumentative. However, she never put me down for having questions. She would listen and try to answer them. When she sensed that she had said all that she could and that I still had questions, she would say something like this: "David, that is a good question. While *you* are searching and reading and praying for the answer, why don't *you* do the things you know you should and not do the things you know you should not?" This became the pattern for my search for truth. Through study, prayer, and keeping the commandments, I found that there are answers to all of

my important questions. I also found that for some questions, continuing faith, patience, and revelation are needed.[1]

As Elder Evans mentioned, we need to be sincere in our efforts to find answers. Elder Evans confessed that some of his questions were more argumentative than sincere. Before I became serious about returning to the Church, many of my questions were more argumentative than sincere, so I didn't get any answers. If we aren't humble, the Spirit won't be able to manifest the truth to us.

But when we do the things that we should be doing, as Elder Evans's mother counseled, the answers will come. Study, prayer, and keeping the commandments helped Elder Evans to receive the answers he was seeking. Those same things helped me to receive my answers when I finally humbled myself and aligned my will with God's.

It's important to note that Elder Evans said some questions require "continuing faith, patience, and revelation." The Lord can't reveal everything to us right now. If He did, there would be no need for faith and our testimonies would not be genuine. When we can't find the answers to our questions because the Lord hasn't revealed them yet, we need to go back to the basics. For example, one of my big concerns about the Book of Mormon was that no one can prove where it took place. But the Lord hasn't revealed that information to us yet, so instead of focusing on where it took place, we need to focus on whether it is true. Focusing on the basics may seem too simple at times, but the gospel is simple. No one has ever left the Church when focusing on the basics.

It's okay to have questions, and all of us will have doubts from time to time. But we should remember the counsel of Elder Uchtdorf: "Doubt your doubts before you doubt your faith."[2] That doesn't mean you can't ask questions about the gospel. But that does mean that before you let the adversary turn you away, remember the foundation on which your faith was built. Think about the experiences you have had that have strengthened your testimony and the times God has answered your prayers. When Oliver Cowdery asked God to confirm something he had already asked Him, Oliver was told, "If you desire a further witness, cast your mind upon the night that you cried unto me in your heart, that you might know concerning the truth of these things. Did I not speak peace to your mind concerning the matter? What greater witness can you have than from God?" (D&C 6:22–23).

If God has already told you that something is true, His answer will not change if you ask again. God is the "same yesterday, today, and forever" (1 Nephi 10:18). His gospel doesn't change. If we think something isn't true anymore, it's because we have decided that it isn't true anymore. God doesn't tell us one day that the prophet is His servant and then change His mind the next day.

If you are struggling with your faith, remember the following tips:

QUESTIONS AND DOUBTS ARE NOT THE SAME

Everyone has questions. At some point everyone has doubts too. However, questions and doubts are not the same.

Questions lead you to earnestly seek answers that will help you build your testimony. Examples of sincere questions include the following: Is the Book of Mormon true? Is the prophet really called of God? Why is tithing a commandment? When you sincerely seek the answers to these questions, God will help you understand these principles, and the Holy Ghost will witness to you that these things are true.

Doubts take away from what you already know to be true. You may have received a witness that the Book of Mormon is true but then hear something negative about it and think maybe it isn't true. We all have doubts from time to time, although some people have bigger doubts than others. The important thing is how you handle your doubts. If you sincerely pray and ask Heavenly Father for answers, He will remind you what you already know. But if you become prideful and think you know better than the Spirit, you will eventually lose your testimony and find yourself on a difficult path that leads you away from Heavenly Father.

Again, heed the counsel of Elder Uchtdorf: "Doubt your doubts before you doubt your faith."[3] If God already gave you an answer, trust Him. God will never lead you astray.

Be Humble

Having humility is one of the most important parts of having faith. If you aren't humble, God can't speak to you. Your heart will be too hard to receive the promptings from the Holy Ghost. Back in 2009 after the missionaries' blessing healed me from the swine flu, I didn't gain a testimony because I wasn't truly humble. I was reading the scriptures, attending sacrament meeting, and praying, but I wasn't humble. My attitude was more of daring God to tell me the Church was true. You never dare God to do anything. And then when the stake president told me I would need a Church court in order to get baptized again, my pride got the best of me and I was offended.

True humility means submitting your will to God's will. If you want God to give you an answer, you need to be willing to accept it and do whatever it takes to follow Him.

Be Prayerful and Allow the Spirit to Speak to You

There's a difference between saying a prayer and being prayerful. Anyone can utter words and say a prayer. If you are prayerful, you are humble and sincere. You truly speak to God and wait for Him to speak to you. In Doctrine and Covenants 112:10, the Lord said, "Be thou humble; and the Lord thy God shall lead thee by the hand, and give thee answers to thy prayers." When you pray with humility and listen for the still, small voice of the Spirit, you will receive your answers.

BE PATIENT

God answers us in His time and when we need to hear the answers most. If the answers don't come right away, keep waiting patiently. If you ask sincerely, God will answer you. It just may not happen right away. No one gains a testimony overnight, and I am no exception. I received answers to my questions over several months. When my testimony did return, it came back all at once, but I still had to go through the process of reading, studying, praying, and having faith that God would someday answer me.

DON'T BE AFRAID TO ASK FOR HELP

God gave us families, friends, and church leaders for a reason. Don't be afraid to ask them for help. When I lost my testimony in 1989, I didn't have many people I could turn to for help. I was the only member of the Church in my family and didn't have many friends as a busy law student. I did turn to my bishop, but he wasn't able to answer my questions and told me not to worry about those things. I don't blame him for this response. He's human and makes mistakes just like the rest of us. Things may have turned out differently if I had trusted friends or other people I could've talked to.

I hope that your situation is different and that you have people you can turn to. If you do, don't be ashamed to go to them. They love you and will be happy to help you. All of us struggle at times, and no one should have to struggle alone.

DON'T BELIEVE EVERYTHING
YOU READ ONLINE

This is a big one. There are tons of anti-Mormon literature online. I know because I've read a lot of it. I have even used most of it to debate members of the Church. Don't believe everything you read online. The internet is a wonderful resource, but you need to be careful. Satan is very good at weaving his lies into truth. You may think you are reading Church doctrine only to find out differently later.

If you are seeking answers online, use trusted sources such as mormon.org and lds.org. If you're chatting with someone online, pay attention to how they make you feel. If you are speaking to someone who is contentious, that's a good indication that they don't have your best interest in mind. Always let the Spirit be your guide. If you have an uncomfortable feeling while reading, stop and pray about it. God will tell you if what you're reading is true.

You Don't Have to Know Everything Right Now

Learning the gospel is a lifelong pursuit. Even the prophet and General Authorities are still learning. If they knew everything, they wouldn't continue studying the scriptures every day. You don't have to know everything right now. Do your best to study the scriptures and learn about the gospel, but don't get overwhelmed with how much you still need to learn.

Would you feed a newborn baby a steak? Even if he managed to swallow it without choking, he wouldn't be able to digest it. While nourishing to an older person, meat would only harm the baby. The Apostle Paul taught us that we need milk before meat (see 1 Corinthians 3:2). Before we can learn deeper doctrine, we need to know the basics.

Faith without Works Is Dead

Earlier this year, Susan and I drove three hours north to Idaho Falls, where I was speaking at a fireside. We were about twenty-three miles away from Idaho Falls when the gas light came on, and the indicator told me that we had twenty-one miles of gas left.

"I have faith that we can make it," Susan said.

We continued to drive, and as the miles passed the gas gauge indicated that we weren't going to make it. Still, Susan was confident. "I have faith we will make it."

We made it to our exit, but we ran out of gas before making it to a gas station and had to walk about a quarter mile to the gas station.

"I had faith we would make it!" Susan said.

"Susan," I said, "faith without gas is dead."

You've probably heard the popular scripture in James 2:17: "Faith without works is dead." Susan no doubt had enough faith, but our works didn't complement our faith. We had hoped that the Lord would help us when we hadn't done enough on our own. We could have stopped at a gas station sooner but chose not to.

When we want the Lord's help, we have to do our part. Belief is essential but not enough. If you want to know if the Church is true, you need to do more than simply have faith that God will tell you. You need to demonstrate your faith by studying the scriptures, attending church, and praying for an answer. Heavenly Father wants to help you, but He also needs to see you doing your part. If He gave us everything we asked for simply because we asked for it, we would end up like a spoiled child without any faith.

Don't Fall Because of the Easiness of the Way

We see examples of people in the scriptures who perished because they thought something was too easy. Isn't that ironic? Don't we want life to be easy and simple? Why do we try to make things so complicated?

In 2 Kings 5 in the Old Testament, we read about Naaman, a commander of the army of Syria, who had leprosy. The prophet Elisha instructed Naaman to bathe in the Jordan River seven times and he would be healed. At first Naaman scoffed at this, thinking it was too simple. How could bathing in the river cure him of his leprosy? Namaan's servant convinced him to give it a try. Miraculously, Namaan was healed.

Fortunately, with a little coaxing, Namaan listened to the prophet's counsel. But not everyone obeys so readily. When the children of Israel were traveling in the desert, God told Moses how to heal those who had been bitten by poisonous snakes (see Numbers 21). Moses was commanded to create a brass serpent, put it on a pole, and then raise it up for all to see. Whoever looked up at it would be healed. Many people looked at the brass serpent and were healed. Others thought it was too simple and foolish. Those people died.

How often do we ignore the prophet's counsel because it seems too easy? How often do we think we can skip our prayers or church meetings or scripture study because they are such simple tasks? In Alma 37, the prophet Alma counseled his son Helaman not to fall because of the easiness of the way: "O my son, do not let us be slothful because of the easiness of the way; for so was it with our fathers; for so was it prepared for them, that if they would look they might live; even so it is with us. The way is prepared, and if we will look we may live forever" (v. 46).

Sometimes members of the Church fall because of the easiness of the way. They think that the simple truths of the gospel are not enough and want more. They want answers to complicated questions, but some of those answers have not yet been revealed to us.

The gospel is simple and easy to understand. The steps to gaining a testimony are simple as well: read, ponder, pray, and wait for an answer from the Spirit (see Moroni 10:3–5). That's it. The formula is so simple that even little children can follow it. Have you ever wondered why children seem to have such pure testimonies? It's because they focus on the basics. They don't understand everything fully, but they don't care. They know that Heavenly Father loves them, and that is enough.

Don't be fooled by the simplicity of the gospel. It may sound too easy, but focus on the basics. The basics—faith, repentance, baptism, and the gift of the Holy Ghost—are the things that will lead you back to Heavenly Father. Don't disregard the basics because they seem too easy. Don't make things more complicated than they have to be.

ALWAYS REMEMBER THAT YOU ARE A CHILD OF GOD

Heavenly Father loves you more than you can comprehend. He wants you to return to Him someday and will do everything in His power to make that happen. In Moses 1:39 the Lord said, "Behold this is my work and my glory—to bring to pass the immortality and eternal life of man." That means that everything Heavenly Father does is for us. Everything He does is for you. All of His efforts and all of His time are spent helping His children return to Him.

God is acutely aware of you. Even when you aren't aware of Him, He is aware of you. He will intervene at the appropriate times to bring you the greatest joy and put you on a path to return to Him.

You may have questions. You may have doubts. But remember what Nephi said: "I know that [God] loveth his children; nevertheless, I do not know the meaning of all things" (1 Nephi 11:17).

You don't have to know everything right now. But know that God loves you. Know that He wants you to return to Him and will do everything He can to help you. Let Him lead you by the hand. He will put you on the right path.

Sometimes you'll have questions that no one can answer. It's okay. Just "be still and know that [He is] God" (Psalm 46:10). Have faith in Him and trust Him. "Look unto [Him] in every thought; doubt not, fear not" (D&C 6:36).

NOTES

1.   David F. Evans, "The Truth of All Things," *Ensign*, Nov. 2017.
2.   Dieter F. Uchtdorf, "Come, Join with Us." *Ensign*, Nov. 2013.
3.   Ibid.

Conclusion

*You can't go back and change the beginning, but you
can start where you are and then change the ending.*[1]

—*James R. Sherman*

I'm so grateful that God gave me a second chance. When I stepped
into the waters of baptism for the second time and saw my old
life flash before me, I knew things had to be different with my
new life. I couldn't break my covenants again, and I had to spend
my life defending the Church with the same vigor I defended my
clients in my law practice. I had to use the lessons learned from the
past twenty-six years to repair my wrongs and move forward on the
path of discipleship.

Three years have now passed. It's hard to believe sometimes
that it's only been three years. My old life feels light years away.
Never in my wildest dreams would I have imagined I'd be where
I am today. I'm living in Utah instead of in Texas. My wife is a
member of the Church instead of a Baptist. I'm teaching classes for
the Church and speaking at firesides instead of teaching against
the Church to other religions. My story was told in general conference, and I was ordained a high priest by an Apostle of the Lord.

All of this happened because God loves me. He never stopped
loving me, even when I turned my back on Him. Even when I was
horrible and tried to destroy His church.

My message to you is that God loves you. He loved you before
you came to Earth and will love you for eternity. Everything He

does is for you. All of His efforts are spent helping you return to Him. At times you may feel unworthy of His love. You may feel like you can't possibly be loved in the state you are in right now. But that's not true. God's love transcends all time and all circumstances. God's love is eternal. He loved you yesterday, He loves you today, and He'll love you forever.

My story is proof of that. I feel like I was one of the vilest of sinners. Yet God still loved me and brought me back. If He can help someone like me, He can help anyone. Don't give up on Him. He'll never give up on you.

My baptism is one of the greatest indications that it's never too late to change. It's never too late to return to God. When I came up out of the waters on that spring morning three years ago, I felt like the prodigal son returning home. It was a long and difficult journey, but I was home and in the arms of my loving father. And then God poured out His love even more and gave me a life I never dreamed possible. It's been incredible. It's been surreal. It's happened because of divine design.

I can't help but wonder what's next. I have no idea what the future holds, but I'm excited. With God, anything is possible.

I have had a trial of faith. And there has been a verdict: God won.

NOTE

1.   James R. Sherman, *Rejection* (Golden Valley, MN: Pathway Books, 1982), 45.

Acknowledgments

Dusty Smith

I would like to thank my wife for supporting her driven husband. I would also like to thank President Dieter Uchtdorf for his love.

Thank you to Kimiko Hammari, who got inside my head and wrote this book.

Also, thank you to Jay and Larna Eubanks for opening up their hearts to us.

A thank you to the 10th Ward in the Rose Park Stake, for all their love and for accepting us with open arms and hearts.

Thank you to Jeanie Humphrey for her endless prayers.

I also want to thank Dean and Jackie Hall for their support. Dean is, and has been, my brother. I also thank Lewis Hall for his guidance and his father's blessings. He is greatly missed.

And, a huge thanks to Mike Robertson, who never gave up on me.

Kimiko Christensen Hammari

Thank you to Dusty Smith for trusting me with his story and helping me to recognize God's hand in my life.

A big thank you to my husband, Dan, for always supporting me in my endeavors.

To my parents, Kerry and Eleanor Christensen, who encouraged an eight-year-old girl who decided she wanted to be an author when she grew up.

ACKNOWLEDGMENTS

To Heather Holm, who has been my mentor and friend for the past twelve years, and to all of the other editors at Cedar Fort who have polished my work over the years.

About the Authors

Dusty Smith

Steve "Dusty" Smith has been an attorney since 1990. He also served in the military, reaching the rank of Lieutenant Colonel. LTC Smith obtained his bachelor of science in public relations from the University of Texas at Austin in 1982 while being a full-time student and working a full-time job. He later obtained his juris doctor from Thomas Cooley Law School. After law school, LTC Smith went into the Army. After leaving active duty, Dusty served three terms as a city councilman in Texas and later served as Acting Chairman of the Dallas, Texas Civil Service Commission.

To contact Dusty, email him at celticmormon@outlook.com.

Kimiko Christensen Hammari

Kimiko Christensen Hammari is the author of nearly twenty books for children and families. She served a mission in Canada and graduated from Brigham Young University with a degree in English. She currently lives in Utah with her family.

Scan to visit

www.brotherdustysmith.com